The Alaska Peninsula

ALASKA GEOGRAPHIC®

Volume 21, Number 1 / 1994

The Alaska Geographic Society

To teach many to better know and more wisely use our natural resources...

Editor
PENNY RENNICK

Production Director
KATHY DOOGAN

Staff Writer
L.J. CAMPBELL

Bookkeeper/Database Manager
VICKIE STAPLES

BOARD OF DIRECTORS
Richard Carlson
Kathy Doogan
Penny Rennick

Robert A. Henning,
President Emeritus

POSTMASTER: Send address changes to

ALASKA GEOGRAPHIC®
P.O. Box 93370
Anchorage, Alaska 99509-3370

ISBN: 1-56661-018-4

**Price to non-members
this issue: $19.95**

PRINTED IN U.S.A.

COVER: *The fishing vessel* Kadiak *plies Alaska Peninsula waters near Castle Cape in the Chignik district. (Jeff Caven)*

PREVIOUS PAGE: *The spires of 4,800-foot Aghileen Pinnacles front the volcanoes of (from left) Pavlov Sister, Pavlov and Little Pavlov, near Cold Bay. (John Sarvis)*

FACING PAGE: *Coastal marshes, such as this one near Port Heiden, typify the Bering Sea side of the Alaska Peninsula. (George Wuerthner)*

ALASKA GEOGRAPHIC® is published quarterly by The Alaska Geographic Society, 639 West Intl. Airport Road, Unit 38, Anchorage, AK 99518. Second-class postage paid at Anchorage, Alaska, and additional mailing offices. Copyright © 1994 by The Alaska Geographic Society. All rights reserved. Registered trademark: Alaska Geographic, ISSN 0361-1353; Key title Alaska Geographic.

THE ALASKA GEOGRAPHIC SOCIETY is a non-profit organization exploring new frontiers of knowledge across the lands of the Polar Rim, putting the geography book back in the classroom, exploring new methods of teaching and learning—sharing in the excitement of discovery in man's wonderful new world north of 51°16'.

SOCIETY MEMBERS receive *ALASKA GEOGRAPHIC®*, a quality publication that devotes each quarterly issue to monographic in-depth coverage of a northern geographic region or resource-oriented subject.

MEMBERSHIP in The Alaska Geographic Society costs $39 per year, $49 to non-U.S. addresses. ($31.20 of the membership fee is for a one-year subscription to *ALASKA GEOGRAPHIC®*.) Order from The Alaska Geographic Society, P.O. Box 93370, Anchorage, AK 99509-3370; telephone (907) 562-0164, fax (907) 562-0479.

SUBMITTING PHOTOGRAPHS: Please write for a list of upcoming topics or other specific photo needs and a copy of our editorial guidelines. We cannot be responsible for unsolicited submissions. Submissions not accompanied by sufficient postage for return by certified mail will be returned by regular mail.

CHANGE OF ADDRESS: The post office does not automatically forward *ALASKA GEOGRAPHIC®* when you move. To ensure continuous service, please notify us six weeks before moving. Send your new address, and, if possible, your membership number or a mailing label from a recent *ALASKA GEOGRAPHIC®* to: The Alaska Geographic Society, P.O. Box 93370, Anchorage, AK 99509-3370.

The Library of Congress has cataloged this serial publication as follows:

Alaska Geographic. v.1-
[Anchorage, Alaska Geographic Society] 1972-
v. ill. (part col.). 23 x 31 cm.
Quarterly
Official publication of The Alaska Geographic Society.
Key title: Alaska geographic, ISSN 0361-1353.

1. Alaska—Description and travel—1959-
—Periodicals. I. Alaska Geographic Society.

F901.A266 917.98'04'505 72-92087

Library of Congress 75[79112] MARC-S

COLOR SEPARATIONS BY:
Graphic Chromatics

PRINTED BY: Hart Press

ABOUT THIS ISSUE: We thank all those who shared their knowledge and personal experiences of life on the Alaska Peninsula. We'd like to note particularly the help of: Don Braun and Roy Skonberg, Chignik; Chick Beckley, Cold Bay; Ret. Lt. Col. Lyman Woodman, Anchorage, for Cold Bay military history; Bobby Galovin and Gale Daniels of Sand Point, and Carol Smith, formerly of Sand Point; Charles Franz, formerly of Nelson Lagoon; Marie Matsuno for help with Ugashik; Cecelia and Emil Christensen, for help with Pilot Point and the upper peninsula; Annie Christensen, Port Heiden; Judy Hurd, King Salmon; Kvichak River set-netter Kevin Scribner of Walla Walla, Wash.; Bob Juettner, Tim Troll, Denby Lloyd and Sharon Boyette of the Aleutians East Borough; Bob Price, Bristol Bay Native Corp.; Nels Anderson, Bristol Bay Economic Development Corp; Glenn Vernon, Lake and Peninsula Borough; Patricia McClenahan, archaeologist, Katmai National Park and Preserve, King Salmon; Debra Corbett, archaeologist, U.S. Fish and Wildlife Service, Anchorage, for shar-ing her work in Chignik Bay; Bill Bright, Peter Pan Seafoods, Seattle; and Pat Partnow, Anchorage, for sharing her doctoral dissertation about the Alutiiq people.

We thank Ric Wilson, Tina Neal and Julie Dumoulin of the U.S. Geological Survey, Ed Bailey of the U.S. Fish and Wildlife Service and Bill Workman, anthropologist with the University of Alaska Anchorage, for reviewing sections of the main text; and Richard Russell, Alaska Department of Fish and Game, King Salmon; and Alan Quimby and other fisheries biologists with ADF&G, Commercial Fisheries Division, Kodiak, who reviewed the fishing chapter.

Many residents of the Alaska Peninsula provided information and reviewed portions of the manuscript. We are grateful for the assistance of these Alaskans: Delores Stokes, Sand Point; Father Maxim Isaac, Chignik Lake; Wayne Mitchell, Chignik Lagoon; Lila Degracia and Dick Sharpe, Chignik; Gary Hennigh, King Cove; Linn Clawson, Nelson Lagoon; Roxanne Shade, Port Heiden; Orin Seybert and Sonny Griechen, Pilot Point; Hazel Nelson, president of Becharof Corp.; Dick Deigh, Egegik; Cynthia Zuelow-Osborne, Bristol Bay Borough; John Knutsen, Naknek; and Susan Savage, resource specialist with the National Park Service.

We appreciate the research of Chris Dau on the staff of Izembek National Wildlife Refuge in preparation of the eelgrass bed diagram.

Writer Bill Sherwonit and photographer Mark Dolan visited several Alaska Peninsula communities while interviewing area residents for a publication on the 20th anniversary of the Bristol Bay Area Health Corp.

We thank Heidi Bohi, economic development coordinator and tourism planner for the Southwest Alaska Municipal Conference, for suggestions on sources of information when we began this project. Staff writer, L.J. Campbell, wrote the main chapter on fishing, and the accounts of the region's communities, with the exception of the Shumagins and Sand Point written by editor Penny Rennick.

Contents

Alaska Peninsula:
The Great Meeting Ground

by Richard P. Emanuel

Editor's note: *In its 20 years of publishing, The Alaska Geographic Society has covered Alaska from many perspectives. Still, some areas have been overlooked, and the lower Alaska Peninsula is one of those areas. Technically, the peninsula extends from the Katmai-Iliamna area southwest to Isanotski Strait at the beginning of the Aleutian chain. Previous issues have dealt with the Katmai and Lake Iliamna areas, so this volume will concentrate on the middle and lower peninsula.*

A frequent contributor to ALASKA GEOGRAPHIC®, *Dick Emanuel is a former hydrologist with the U.S. Geological Survey.*

Autumn in the eelgrass beds of Izembek Lagoon is a time of noise and tumult. A quarter-million migrating birds convene each fall in and around the lagoon at the Alaska Peninsula's tip. They feed and rest for the flight to wintering grounds in the south from summer nesting areas throughout Alaska, Asia and the North Pacific. Emperor geese, Canada geese, dabbling ducks and shorebirds of all descriptions meet in clamorous congregation.

Virtually all the world's black brant, a small coastal goose, transit Izembek National Wildlife Refuge.

Many species visit Izembek twice a year, in spring and fall. Others are year-round residents, including a unique population of tundra swans which do not migrate beyond the region. Near year's end, gray whales skirt the Alaska Peninsula en route from Bering Sea feeding grounds to warm breeding lagoons off Mexico. In April and May, the leviathans retrace their route, shepherding 3-ton calves.

The Alaska Peninsula is not only a meeting ground for wildlife. Geologically, it is part of the Aleutian volcanic arc, produced by the collision of two of the earth's great crustal plates. It is also a cultural meeting ground, where the Pacific Eskimos of the Gulf of Alaska meet their cousins, the Aleuts of the Aleutian Islands, and where both Native groups met first the Russians and then the Americans.

The Alaska Peninsula swings in a graceful arc some 460 miles southwest from mainland Alaska to the Aleutian Islands. The peninsula's spine is the Alaska-Aleutian Range. Studded with volcanoes, the range divides the land into two provinces. The Bristol Bay side features rolling tundra drained by streams and lakes rich with salmon. The Pacific coast is indented with misty bays and rugged fiords with short, rushing streams. Rocky headlands in many places face craggy islands offshore.

The whole of the peninsula is infamous for its weather. The polar maritime climate is moderate in temperature but windy, cloudy and subject to storms. Cold Bay, about 40 miles from the peninsula's tip, receives

Pink and silver salmon form a dark cloud in this creek entering Baralof Bay on the east side of Unga Island, largest of the Shumagins. A forest of petrified Miocene-age metasequoia trees is exposed along a quarter mile of Unga's north coast. Scientists think these 15-million-to-20-million-year-old trees were petrified shortly after they were engulfed by mud flows from an ancient volcano. (Dee Randolph)

precipitation on 200 days in an average year. It enjoys just 12 clear days a year and has cloud cover 90 percent of the time. The climate improves to the north. King Salmon has cloud cover 76 percent of the time and enjoys 55 clear days a year.

The Pacific is warmer than the Bering Sea and it pumps more moisture into the air. The steep terrain of the Pacific side ensures plenty of fog, rain and snow. Annual precipitation near Chignik, on the Pacific coast, is 160 inches. The Bristol Bay coastal plain north of Port Moller receives just 20 inches a year. The mountains are lower with more open passes south of Port Moller. There, the warm and the cold seas battle constantly and both sides of the peninsula share a common, wet climate.

Nearly all that happens on the Alaska Peninsula owes something to the sea. It sustains the wildlife and the people and has shaped the region's history. But the land has its own wonders, too, from exploding volcanoes to ancient village sites to the world's densest gathering of bears.

Where Crustal Plates Collide

The story of the Alaska Peninsula stretches back roughly 200 million years to the Jurassic period, the age of dinosaurs. Even before then, limestone and other rocks that were to become part of the peninsula were laid down in warm seas, at about 15 degrees north. Magnetic traces in these rocks show they were rafted northward with the slow, jostling drift of plates of the earth's crust. By Middle Jurassic time, 160 to 185 million years ago, they had docked against North America and reached the peninsula's present latitude, 55 degrees to 59 degrees north.

The collision of crustal plates that plastered these ancient rocks against North America also melted great volumes of rock. Along the collision front, bodies of molten rock, or magma, formed deep within the crust. Where magma squeezed to the surface, volcanic vents arose. Geologists call such a system a volcanic arc.

As time passed, the buried magma cooled and solidified into granite and similar kinds of rock. The collision that formed the volcanic arc soon lifted the volcanoes and granites to form the core of a mountain chain. The Alaska-Aleutian Range began to erode. Rivers washed weathered granite and volcanic debris into the sea, where the sediments formed new rock. One sedimentary rock unit formed in this way is called the Naknek Formation. It occurs throughout the Alaska Peninsula and southcentral Alaska as far north as Talkeetna. It abounds with fossil mollusks from the Late Jurassic sea.

When the Jurassic period closed 140 million years ago, the granite core of the Alaska-Aleutian Range had been much eroded, according to Ric Wilson of the U.S. Geological Survey. What had been high, jagged mountains had become lowlands and rolling hills. During the succeeding Cretaceous period, the Naknek Formation itself was eroded and its sediments were recycled into younger rocks.

Cape Douglas and neighboring Kamishak Bay mark the northeastern boundary of the Alaska Peninsula. British seafarer Capt. James Cook named the promontory for his friend Dr. John Douglas, canon of Windsor. (Steven Seiller)

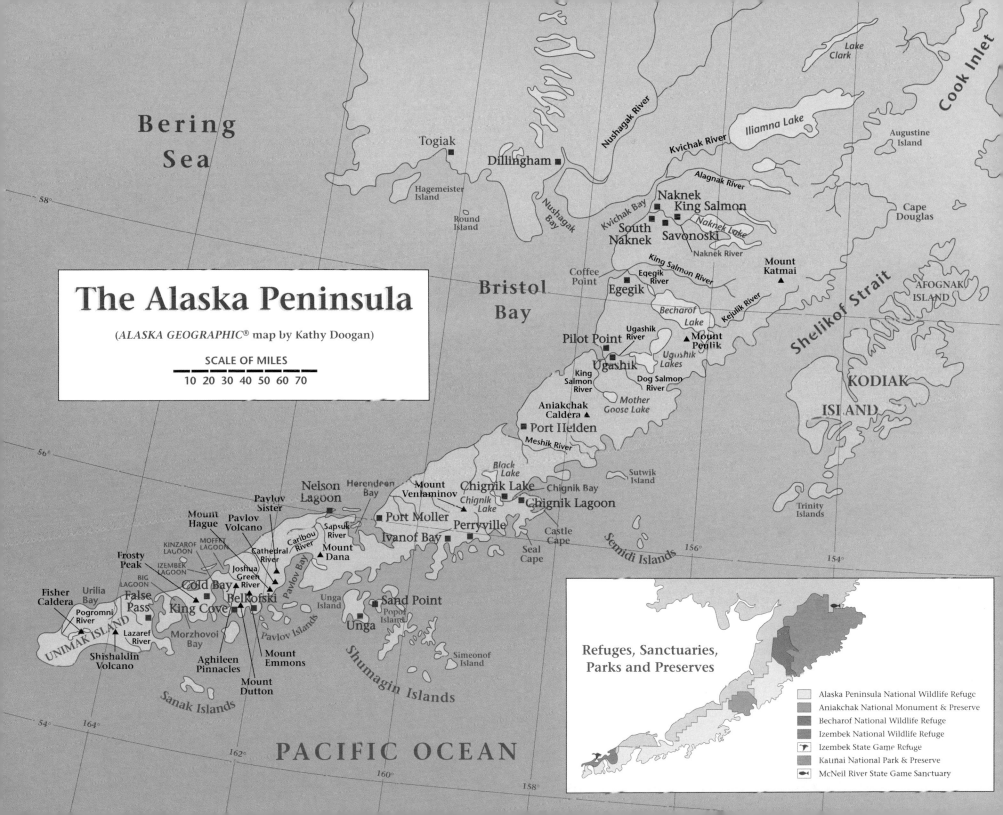

The Alaska Peninsula

(*ALASKA GEOGRAPHIC*® map by Kathy Doogan)

SCALE OF MILES

10 20 30 40 50 60 70

Bering Sea

PACIFIC OCEAN

Cook Inlet

Lake Clark

Togiak

Dillingham

Hagemeister Island

Round Island

Nushagak River

Nushagak Bay

Kvichak Bay

Iliamna Lake

Kvichak River

Alagnak River

Augustine Island

Cape Douglas

Naknek
King Salmon
South Naknek
Savonoski
Naknek Lake
Naknek River

Mount Katmai

Shelikof Strait

AFOGNAK ISLAND

Bristol Bay

Coffee Point

King Salmon River

Egegik
Egegik River

Becharof Lake

Kejulik River

Mount Peulik

Pilot Point
Ugashik River

Ugashik
King Salmon River

Dog Salmon River

Ugashik Lakes

Mother Goose Lake

KODIAK ISLAND

Aniakchak Caldera ▲

Port Heiden

Meshik River

Black Lake

Chignik Lake

Chignik Bay

Sutwik Island

Nelson Lagoon

Herendeen Bay

Mount Veniaminof

Chignik Lake

Chignik Lagoon

Castle Cape

Trinity Islands

Pavlov Sister

Mount Hague

Pavlov Volcano

KINZAROF LAGOON

MOFFET LAGOON

IZEMBEK LAGOON

Caribou River

Sapsuk River

Cathedral River

Mount Dana

Port Moller

Perryville

Ivanof Bay

Seal Cape

Semidi Islands

Frosty Peak

Joshua Green River

Pavlov Bay

Sand Point

Fisher Caldera

Urilia Bay

BIG LAGOON

Cold Bay

Belkofski

Unga Island

Popof Island

Pogromni River

False Pass

King Cove

Pavlov Islands

Unga

UNIMAK ISLAND

Lazaref River

Morzhovoi Bay

Simeonof Island

Shishaldin Volcano

Aghileen Pinnacles

Mount Emmons

Mount Dutton

Sanak Islands

Shumagin Islands

Refuges, Sanctuaries, Parks and Preserves

- ☐ Alaska Peninsula National Wildlife Refuge
- ☐ Aniakchak National Monument & Preserve
- ☐ Becharof National Wildlife Refuge
- ☐ Izembek National Wildlife Refuge
- ⚐ Izembek State Game Refuge
- ☐ Katmai National Park & Preserve
- ⚐ McNeil River State Game Sanctuary

58°

56°

54°

164°

162°

160°

158°

156°

154°

Numerous glaciers and snow fields cover the high peaks of the Alaska-Aleutian Range. This unnamed glacier flows from 7,000-foot Mount Douglas. (Chlaus Lotscher)

Roughly 80 million years ago, in the Late Cretaceous period, another cycle of uplift and erosion began on the peninsula. Again, existing rocks were eroded, washed away and redeposited to form new sedimentary rocks. This cycle continued for millions of years, then fresh volcanic rocks appeared. A new volcanic arc was forming on the Alaska Peninsula.

"That arc really started to kick off about 40 to 42 million years ago," says Wilson, "and that's a real key time. That's about the date of the bend in the Hawaiian-Emperor seamount chain, when the Pacific plate's direction of motion changed significantly."

The Hawaiian-Emperor seamounts are a chain of volcanoes built atop a hot spot, a sort of blow torch in the earth's interior. As the Pacific plate moves across the hot spot, lava wells up in a line of successive volcanoes. Some 42 million years ago, the line bent, recording a shift in the direction of plate motion. Along the plate's northern boundary, the same shift may have ignited a new volcanic arc on the Alaska Peninsula.

The volcanic arc that kicked off 42 million years ago is called the Meshik arc, after the Meshik River where it was first recognized. "The bulk of the activity took place between 30 and 40 million years ago," Wilson says. "Then it seemed to wind down. It was pretty much through by about 25 million years ago."

The Meshik arc was closely related to the modern Aleutian arc. Both were born of the ongoing collision which forces the Pacific plate down under North America. Relative quiet prevailed for about 10 million years after the Meshik arc lapsed into silence.

"Then about 10 to 15 million years ago, the Aleutian arc got started," Wilson says. "It has a slightly different orientation." The modern arc has been rotated clockwise with respect to the older arc. The Aleutian arc begins on the west side of Cook Inlet, runs down the Alaska Peninsula and through the Aleutian Islands. It is one of the most active segments of the Pacific "Ring of Fire." Pavlov Volcano, near the peninsula's tip, is among the most active volcanoes on earth. During the last 200 years, it has erupted at least 30 times.

The glacial epoch, or Ice Age, which began 2 to 3 million years ago wrought profound changes on the Alaska Peninsula. Before the Ice Age, the southern peninsula was probably a series of volcanic islands, like the Aleutians. Great glaciers built sand and gravel bridges which joined some of the islands together and linked them with the mainland. Pavlov Volcano was probably added to the peninsula in this way.

The end of the Ice Age, 10,000 years ago, may have brought profound events, too. Tom Miller of the Alaska Volcano Observatory has studied Alaska volcanoes for 30 years. One of his interests is calderas, huge craters formed by ground collapse after great eruptions of volcanic debris. A 1981 catalog of the world's largest eruptions since the Ice Age listed 17 great eruptions but only one in the Aleutian arc, the caldera-forming eruption in Katmai, in 1912. Evidence today points to at least six post-glacial, caldera-forming blasts on the Alaska Peninsula alone, Miller says.

The 1912 cataclysm in what is now Katmai National Park was one of the three greatest eruptions in recorded history. The blast

Erosion by water of volcanic ash and its leached minerals is for the most part all that remains of the Valley of 10,000 Smokes' formerly steaming vents. After the 1912 eruption of Novarupta, the valley's streams were buried under hundreds of feet of hot ash in places. The trapped water found its way to the surface and vented as steam, giving a name to the valley, now within Katmai National Park, and leaving behind leached mineral deposits. (Charlie Crangle)

formed Novarupta caldera plus a second caldera, six miles away, when the summit of Mount Katmai also collapsed. Less well-known than its neighbors, Kaguyak crater, in the park's northeast corner, is a third, post-glacial caldera. Kaguyak is 1.6 miles across and contains a lake with a central cinder cone, reminiscent of Oregon's Crater Lake.

The region's most spectacular caldera may be Aniakchak, in the peninsula's heart. Six miles across and 3,000 feet deep, it has undergone two major eruptions and countless small ones since the retreat of the glaciers. During the second blast, 3,400 years ago, red-hot slurries of volcanic gas, ash and larger debris spilled from the crater and flowed 50 miles over rolling tundra toward the Bering Sea. To the east, incandescent clouds of debris flowed into the Pacific Ocean.

Black Peak, 35 miles south of Aniakchak, is a relatively small caldera, just under two miles across. Thirty-five miles southwest of Black Peak there rises the immense bulk of Mount Veniaminov, with its summit caldera 6 miles across, 8,000 feet above sea level. The huge summit crater is filled to overflowing with glacial ice. During eruptions in 1983-84 and in 1993, ash and lava spewed from a cone projecting through the ice.

The spate of large, post-glacial eruptions on the peninsula, plus others on nearby Aleutian Islands, has Miller and other scientists

Night on the Lava Flow

By Richard P. Emanuel

Editor's note: *In July 1993, Mount Veniaminov began to erupt for at least the 10th time since 1838. As of November, the modest event was continuing but had produced only a light ashfall in Port Heiden along with an occasional light show for residents of Perryville. That was enough to trigger in writer Dick Emanuel recollections of the volcano's most recent previous eruption, 10 years earlier, when he worked for the U.S. Geological Survey.*

Geologist Tom Miller inspects a fumarole venting steam from the cooling lava flow. Behind Miller looms the dirty white ice of the melt-pit wall. (Richard P. Emanuel, USGS)

The geothermal tea being brewed on the ground was almost ready when the big Coast Guard helicopter burst into view from behind the volcanic cone. The chopper banked with a loud *throp! throp! throp!* and swung into a lazy orbit above us. We'd been expecting them, more or less. But as I glanced at the warming tea, it crossed my mind that our rescuers could have had slightly better timing.

A moment later, I was on my feet. I rummaged in my pocket for the aerial flare I'd been toying with for the last 20 hours, unscrewed the protective base, pointed the tube skyward, averted my head and yanked the cord, *bang!* The concussion stung my hand. The orange flare arced skyward, there to join one launched by Tom Miller, my companion in scientific adventure. Our pilot was inside his recalcitrant helicopter, talking by radio with the Coast Guard crew, arranging our rescue from Veniaminov volcano.

That was in August 1984. I worked for the U.S. Geological Survey then. Among my professional interests were the interactions of volcanoes and glaciers, which was how I wound up marooned on a still-cooling lava flow surrounded by ice, a mile and a half above sea level.

Mount Veniaminov, a large volcano in the central Alaska Peninsula, is a stratocone, made up of alternating layers of lava and ash. Built by succeeding eruptions during tens of thousands of years, it has grown to 100 cubic miles in volume. About 3,700 years ago, in a cataclysmic explosion, Veniaminov blew its top. The summit area then collapsed to form a caldera 6 miles across. As the crater cooled, 8,000 feet above sea level, snow and ice began to accumulate. Glacial ice gradually filled the caldera and began to spill through gaps in the rim. Eruptions beneath the ice later raised volcanic welts, including a cone which now protrudes several hundred feet above the glacier.

Veniaminov has been rather active in historic times. Four eruptions were reported between 1838 and 1892. In 1930, Father Bernard Hubbard scaled Veniaminov and observed the cone within the caldera. He found it "packed in ice and smoking... now and then coughing out black ashes over the surrounding white snows." The volcano sputtered to life again in 1939, 1944 and 1956.

Word of a new eruption came in June 1983. Residents of Perryville, on the Pacific coast 20 miles from the volcano, saw dark puffs of ash during the day. At night, through the near-solstice twilight, the mountaintop glowed an otherworldly red. Tom Miller, of the U.S.Geological Survey, decided to check the reports. He asked me to join the effort and I eagerly agreed.

Flying to Veniaminov, 480 miles southwest of Anchorage, a steady parade of snow-capped volcanoes marched beneath the wings of our light plane. As we approached our destination, we saw a dark plume of ash rising from a cone, surrounded by blackened ice. Rhythmic explosions in the top of the cone tossed incandescent lava into the air. Days later, a lava flow started down the southwest flank of the cone. Where lava met ice, columns of steam arose and a melt-pit formed in the glacier. Jet-black ash soon blanketed the 30 square miles of the caldera. By mid-July, the pit was at least a quarter-mile wide and nearly a mile long, with cliffs 200 to 300 feet high. A meltwater lake covered the pit's bottom and a lava delta was growing into the lake. By August, 2.5 billion cubic feet of ice had melted.

The eruption waned in mid-August, then in October, the lava flow resumed. Activity subsided again in March 1984, and by April, the lava flow had ceased. Veniaminov seemed calm enough by summer to permit work on the ground, so Miller and I drew up

During the 1983-84 eruption of Mount Veniaminov, lava melted a pit in the glacial ice that fills the volcano's summit caldera. In this photo from July 13, 1983, black ash blankets the mountaintop glacier. Layers of ash from previous eruptions are exposed in the ice of the melt-pit wall. Also visible is the arched entrance to a subglacial tunnel through which some of the melt-water drained. The bottom of the melt-pit was first covered with water but lava flows gradually filled much of the pit. Roughly 2.5 billion cubic feet of ice melted, creating a pit nearly a mile long, 1/4 mile to 1/2 mile wide and 200 feet to 300 feet deep. Veniaminov erupted again beginning in June 1993. This eruption, strikingly similar to the event of a decade earlier, was continuing as of November 1993. (Richard P. Emanuel, USGS)

plans. Tom was keen to sample the lava, while I was anxious to survey the melt-pit. In August, we gathered our gear and flew to Port Heiden, 60 miles northeast of the volcano, where we met our helicopter.

Fog and clouds greeted us on our first morning in Port Heiden, but Miller, an old peninsula hand, squinted up and pronounced that the overcast was thin. Taking off, our pilot felt his way around and up through patches of dense cloud. Soon, we broke into crystal blue sky and ran for the volcano. We rose to clear the jagged rim of the caldera then floated out into sun-filled space.

Miller's voice crackled over the intercom. "I'd like to sample the lava before we start surveying."

We flew to the cone then spiraled down toward the base, where the lava flow flattened out. Feeling for a landing spot among the rubble of fresh rock, our pilot set down and cut the engine.

As I stepped off the helicopter skid onto the dark, blocky lava, I felt a little like Buzz Aldrin, the second man on the moon, to Tom Miller's Neil Armstrong. For close to an hour, Miller and I scrambled over the lava, looked at structures in the flow, knocked off samples, took photographs, made sketches and notes. The rocks were warm to the touch and steam rose here and there from clefts in the lava. I had a glass thermometer in a protective metal sheath tied to a nylon string, and I thrust it into a steaming crack. After a minute,

I pulled it out. The cord was singed, the glass was shattered.

After our brief reconnaissance, we regrouped at the helicopter. We stowed our samples and gear, climbed into the ship and strapped in. The pilot flipped his switches and did what pilots do. The turbine rose in pitch. But there comes a point in the start-up of a Jet Ranger when the whine of the turbine is suddenly answered by a low *whompf!* from deep within the engine. Not this time. The pilot shut down again, flipped switches off, then on, then tried again. Again. Again.

We unstrapped ourselves and climbed out. The pilot soon figured out what was wrong. It was altitude more than ash, but it couldn't be fixed with the tools and parts on hand.

We were not worried. It was midday. We'd use the radio to relay word to our mechanic, in Port Heiden. The helicopter company had another ship nearby. They'd fly the mechanic up and we'd all be back at the lodge for supper. Only no one returned our radio calls. Hmm.

We were parked near the base of a cone that rose at our back several hundred feet. We were down in a crater and the whole thing was atop a mountain. Local plane traffic mostly detoured around the volcano and the odd jet at 35,000 feet didn't seem to hear us. We could activate our emergency beacon but we were reluctant to trigger a major search. So we got out our survival gear and took stock. We were in no immediate danger, unless the

LEFT: Geologist Tom Miller scrambles over the bouldery surface of the 1983-84 lava flow. Veniaminov's lava is typically classified as basaltic andesite with a lower silica content than rhyolite. The lava has a moderate viscosity or fluidity and flows with moderate ease, which makes for eruptions characterized by only mild explosions. Layers of dark ash from previous eruptions are exposed in the ice wall above Miller. (Richard P. Emanuel, USGS)

BELOW: The morning after their night on Veniaminov's lava flow, Tom Miller (left) and pilot Mike Wilkerson inspect their camping spot while they await the U.S. Coast Guard. (Richard P. Emanuel, USGS)

active eruption resumed, and that was unlikely within the next day or two.

True, steam was blasting from the top of the cone, but it had been doing that for months. Ever the alert volcanologist, Miller soon noticed a pattern: Steam would roar from the cone for 20 minutes, then cease for 20 minutes. When the steam-jet was on, the ground shook.

Miller and I roamed a little farther afield on the lava flow, but we were reluctant to stray too far. We dipped into our ample lunches and chatted quietly. As shadows lengthened, we eyed spots of level ground. At last the sun sank below the caldera rim. The ice around us seemed to draw closer. Slowly, silently, the silver moon floated higher in the pale blue sky.

There was no danger of hypothermia on Mount Veniaminov's lava flows that night. We arranged our foillike emergency blankets on patches of soft ash and threw down our sleeping bags. After five minutes, my back was uncomfortably hot. I rolled onto my left side. After five more minutes, I rolled onto my stomach. Five more minutes, onto my right side. I spun all night, like a leg of lamb on a rotisserie. Now and then, a gust of wind would lightly season me with a sprinkling of gritty ash. Miller later described our experience as akin to sleeping on a full-length hot pad under a Boeing 747 while someone turned the engines on and off at 20-minute intervals.

We rose the next morning expecting some kind of rescue. We would have been reported overdue, a search would be on. The weather looked fine where we were but we knew that clouds could hamper the search below.

We stowed our sleeping bags, ate a light breakfast and began to brew tea over a handy fumarole when help arrived in force, a big military helicopter and a C-130 plane loaded with emergency locator gear. Both were white with the bold, red diagonal of the U.S. Coast Guard.

As the rescue helicopter dropped toward the lava, it seemed to dwarf our own ship. The big chopper hovered noisily just above ground level while we scrambled over and threw our packs and then ourselves through the door. Several guardsmen hopped out to help us. Then they started to shove in hunks of lightweight lava the size of television sets.

"How old is this rock?" one shouted to Miller.

He shrugged. "Two months," he shouted back.

A minute later, as I watched through the open door, the lava flow fell away and our Jet Ranger dwindled. It shrank to the size of a toy before the door slid shut and we turned toward Sand Point, 70 miles to the southeast. Behind us, the cone steamed away, oblivious to our departure. We crossed the jagged caldera rim and the sea shone in the distance, a mile and a half below us, shimmering blue beneath the dazzling sun.

The entire Alaska Peninsula is renowned for its brown bear populations, with the highest concentrations along the coastal areas of Katmai National Park and Becharof National Wildlife Refuge. This bruin family was photographed near Cape Aklek in the Becharof refuge. (John Bauman)

wondering: Are they a coincidence? Certainly, the Aleutian arc is studded with volcanoes, some old but many quite young. The Alaska Peninsula alone has two dozen or more active volcanic centers, an average of one every 20 miles along its mountainous spine.

"It's very striking that we have these fairly old volcanoes," Miller says, "and yet in the last 10,000 years, so many of them have had caldera-forming eruptions. Well, what happened 10,000 years ago? One thing that happened was the glaciers retreated." The melting of billions of tons of ice could have relieved pressure on magma chambers deep in the crust. The drop in pressure may have triggered explosive eruptions. But the idea is speculation.

"The ice was off, and that's a lot of weight," Miller says. "Whether this was related, I don't know. A slight change in plate movement could perhaps do this, too." The flurry of great, post-glacial explosions on the peninsula remains for now a puzzle.

A Confluence of Cultures

The volcanic cataclysms which shook the Alaska Peninsula during the last 10,000 years must in many cases have been witnessed by human beings. Ancestral Native Americans migrated from Asia to Alaska during the Ice Age across a broad lowland called the Bering Land Bridge. The land was exposed when sea level dropped as more and more water was locked up in continental glaciers. Throughout generations, the first Alaskans spread into the landscape, often in pursuit of mammoths, bison and other game.

Humans reached the Alaska Peninsula at least 9,000 years ago, according to University of Oregon archaeologist Don Dumond. Signs of their occupation have been unearthed at Ugashik Narrows, a promontory separating the two Ugashik Lakes.

Archaeological artifacts suggest that the earliest Alaskans shared a common culture, close to the one they brought from Asia. By about 6,000 years ago, inhabitants of different regions had begun to evolve divergent ways of life. On the Alaska Peninsula, mountains formed a boundary between two developing cultures. People on the Bristol Bay side depended chiefly on salmon and used tools and weapons like those of coastal people elsewhere in southwestern Alaska. On the Pacific side, where the rugged terrain was less hospitable, people turned to the sea. They relied on marine mammals — seals, whales, sea lions and sea otters — and on deep-sea fish. They developed boats, tools and techniques that allowed them to hunt and fish in the open sea and gave rise to both the region's Pacific Eskimos and Aleuts.

This ancient maritime culture is preserved in archaeological sites along Shelikof Strait. Early Pacific Eskimos spread around Kodiak and Afognak islands, down the peninsula's Pacific coast and perhaps into the Aleutian Islands, as well as northeastward toward Prince William Sound. By 4,500 years ago, their descendents had evolved a distinctive Aleut culture in the southern peninsula and in the Aleutians, while Pacific Eskimos of the northern peninsula and elsewhere had developed what is called the Kodiak Tradition.

About 2,000 years ago, influences from mainland Alaska began to spread down the Alaska Peninsula. The earlier culture on the

Bering Sea side had been supplanted by 1000 A.D., and both sides of the northern peninsula shared a unified, Pacific Eskimo culture. The wave of influence broke in the southern peninsula, however, and the Aleuts continued to evolve largely on their own.

A number of archaeological sites on the peninsula testify to this long story of human occupation. The Ugashik lakes and river have been used more or less continuously for 9,000 years. Hot springs near Port Moller were probably used by early Aleuts 4,000 years ago; the site was intermittently occupied for 3,000 years. Today, Bristol Bay fishermen use area hot springs to escape inclement weather. Archaeological sites from about 1,000 years ago suggest that Aleuts seasonally harvested the rich wildlife of Izembek Lagoon. One

Izembek excavation has yielded a large, partly earth-covered house, 25 feet to 30 feet across, with boulder walls and a roof framework of whale jawbones.

In 1741, when Vitus Bering led the first Russian voyage to Alaska, Aleuts occupied the Aleutian Islands and southern Alaska Peninsula. Pacific Eskimo groups had settled the northern peninsula, as well as Kodiak Island and areas north and east to Prince William Sound. Because their cultures were so closely related and the artifacts they left were so similar, the boundary between past Aleuts and Pacific Eskimos is hard for archaeologists

to draw. Today, on the basis of language, the Eskimo/Aleut boundary is generally drawn through Port Moller, placing the peninsula north of Port Moller in Eskimo territory and the land to the south, including the Shumagin Islands, in Aleut country. Although anthropologists state that residents of communities north of Port Moller speak a Yup'ik Eskimo dialect, Alutiiq, people in these communities generally call themselves Aleuts.

The Land and Its Recent History

On the return leg of his voyage to Alaska, Vitus Bering paused in the Shumagin Islands to inter a sailor who had died of scurvy. The first Russian ship to visit the Alaska Peninsula proper probably wintered offshore in 1761. Within 25 years, Russian fur traders had erected outposts on the peninsula, along Shelikof Strait. Fur-bearing mammals, especially sea otters, were the magnet that drew them. Fur traders were quickly followed by Russian Orthodox missionaries, who sought to convert the Natives.

To exploit Alaska's rich ocean resources, the Russian American Co., appointed by the Russian crown, forced Eskimo and Aleut hunters into servitude. Natives were often resettled in new areas. Belkofski is one village founded in this way. Aleuts were brought to the site, 12 miles east of present-day King Cove, to harvest the otters of the nearby Sandman Reefs, in 1823.

Fur trading was well-established throughout the peninsula by the early 1800s. Natives traded sea otter pelts and other furs for food, clothing and other essentials. Many grew dependent on the Russians.

After the United States purchased Alaska in 1867, the Alaska Commercial Co. assumed control of Russian American Co. holdings, including trading posts on the Alaska

Peninsula. Sea otters had been nearly wiped out in the region by the close of the 19th century, and the primary industry shifted from fur to fishing.

In the 1880s, salteries and canneries sprang up in Sand Point, Ugashik and Pilot Point. Typically, Chinese crews were brought up from San Francisco to work in the plants each summer. In Port Heiden, Scandinavian settlers and Natives developed a codfishery, followed by a salmon saltery around 1900. Similar developments occurred in Port Moller and Herendeen Bay, as well as in Chignik Bay on the Pacific coast. Near the peninsula's tip, King Cove began as a salmon cannery in 1911. Today, it is the largest community on the peninsula, although it is not as large as Sand Point, in the nearby Shumagin Islands.

Sand Point is the region's largest community. It is the seat of the Aleutians East Borough, which includes the southern peninsula and the Aleutian Islands from Akutan east. The Lake and Peninsula Borough, based in King Salmon, governs the northern peninsula, except for a strip along Shelikof Strait which is part of the Kodiak Island Borough.

Sand Point emerged in the 1880s as a supply point for ships sailing between San Francisco and codfishing grounds off Russia. In 1884, gold was discovered on neighboring Unga Island. Along with Unga village on Unga Island, Sand Point briefly served as a supply center for miners and prospectors. Gold was mined from the beach near the present-day Sand Point airport. The area's mining boom had passed by World War I, but not before $3 million in gold was dug from Unga Island's Apollo Mine.

During World War II, the U.S. Army Air Corps established Fort Randall on the shores of Cold Bay. Up to 40,000 troops were stationed here at the height of the Aleutian campaign. Smaller outposts were scattered farther up the peninsula while the Shumagins were used for rest and recreation. Shortly after the war, Fort Randall was abandoned, although the large airstrip was maintained, first by Reeve Aleutian Airways, then the Federal Aviation Administration and finally the State of Alaska. It now serves the town of Cold Bay, a regional transportation hub whose residents are mostly airline and government workers.

Today, as it has always been, the sea is the wellspring of the peninsula's economy. The largest sockeye or red salmon run in the world is the Bristol Bay run, and it is largely sustained by peninsula streams. The waterways drain rolling tundra plains and offer plenty of pools and riffles for spawning and rearing salmon. Most Pacific-side streams are steeper and offer more limited sockeye habitat, although Black and Chignik lakes are among the notable exceptions.

Chum, silver, pink and king salmon also spawn in peninsula streams. Chum use streams on both sides of the peninsula while silvers concentrate in the Ugashik, Chignik and Meshik river systems. Kings find favorable habitat in the Ugashik River and its tributaries and in several rivers which debouch into Port Heiden. Pinks spawn in great numbers in Chignik Bay and in the lower Ugashik River. Lake trout, Dolly Varden and trophy-size arctic grayling also thrive in peninsula streams, while halibut, crab and shrimp are taken offshore.

Walrus haul out at Cape Seniavin, northeast of Port Moller near where the Muddy River enters the Bering Sea. This haul-out is used mostly in spring and fall by the same males that also gather at Round Island and Cape Pierce on the north shore of Bristol Bay. In 1993, there were about 8,000 to 10,000 walrus using Bristol Bay waters. (John Sarvis)

Aniakchak Caldera

By Bill Sherwonit

Editor's note: *In 1988, Bill Sherwonit visited Aniakchak caldera, heart of one of the least visited units of the national park system. Bill, from Anchorage, is a noted free-lance writer and frequent contributor to ALASKA GEOGRAPHIC®.*

Flying into Aniakchak caldera, there's an immediate and over-whelming sense of desolation. Left behind is the green, living tundra. In its place is a black, brown and gray otherworld of cinder cones, lava flows and explosion pits.

Bleak. Barren. Lifeless.

First impressions can, of course, be quite misleading. Though much of Aniakchak caldera does indeed resemble a moonscape, closer inspection shows this volcanic crater to be far from lifeless.

In summer, scattered meadows of grass and wildflowers brighten the landscape with greens, yellows, reds and purples.

Algae-rich Surprise Lake supports myriad aquatic invertebrates, a resident population of Dolly Varden char and a substantial run of sockeye salmon.

Bald eagles roost on the caldera rim, caribou roam the crater's expansive flatlands and brown bears come to feed on salmon in late summer and early fall.

One species not normally found inside the crater, however, is *Homo sapiens*. During summer 1993, for example, fewer than

A campsite overlooks Surprise Lake in the caldera's northeastern corner. Marshes at both ends of the 2-and-1/2-mile-long lake provide nesting habitat for arctic terns, glaucous-winged and mew gulls, among others, and shorebirds such as semipalmated plovers and spotted sandpipers. (Bill Sherwonit)

20 people camped in Aniakchak. Overnight visitors included four National Park Service researchers, two geologists, five hikers and four rafters. Flightseers also land in the caldera occasionally, but their stays are usually measured in minutes or hours.

Aniakchak caldera, 425 miles southwest of Anchorage, is the highlight of 580,000-acre Aniakchak National Monument and Preserve. The monument is bordered on two sides by Alaska Peninsula National Wildlife Refuge, on another by the Pacific Ocean and on the final side by lowlands fringing Bristol Bay.

Few signs of human use mark the caldera's fragile interior. Even

footprints are rare; most visitors don't stay long enough to make tracks. In recent years, the caldera has been used primarily as a starting point for float trips down the Aniakchak River, which offers Class II to Class IV whitewater — Class VI is the most difficult — rafting on its upper 13 miles. The river then meanders slowly through tundra lowlands for its remaining 14 miles before draining into Aniakchak Bay on the Pacific side.

Discovered in 1922 by a U.S. Geological Survey team led by R.H. Sargent, a topographic engineer, and W.R. Smith, Aniakchak is part of the Pacific Ocean's "Ring of Fire." The

caldera is unusual because its features aren't covered by ice, water or thick vegetation.

Aniakchak caldera was created about 3,500 years ago by the collapse of a large volcano that once reached 7,000 feet, following an eruption that was "very big, far larger than Mount St. Helens," says Tom Miller of the Alaska Volcano Observatory. The remaining rim rises up to 2,500 feet above the crater floor, at elevations of 3,000 to 4,500 feet.

Miller, who has visited Aniakchak more than 10 times during the past two decades, says the volcanic peak "erupted catastrophically" because of an immense gas build-up in a magma chamber beneath it. Once released by the explosion, an estimated 15 to 30 cubic kilometers (about 3 to 6 cubic miles) of gas-rich molten rock and ash spewed out of the ground; by contrast, Mount St. Helens sent out 1 cubic kilometer of material.

Roaring down the mountain at speeds of up to 100 mph, the pyroclastic cloud wiped out everything in its path for a

distance of up to 35 miles, while covering an area of more than 50,000 square miles.

"Undoubtedly, ash from the eruption circled the globe," Miller says. "We've traced deposits almost to the North Slope."

Aniakchak's massive eruption created a huge subsurface void, causing the mountain to cave in on itself and form the caldera.

Aniakchak is still considered active and most recently erupted in 1931, depositing ash on villages up to 45 miles distant. Explosions were heard 20 miles away and a 5-mile-wide mass of floating pumice was discovered in Bristol Bay, north of the volcano.

Exploring the crater a month after the 1931 eruption, renowned Jesuit priest and geologist Father Bernard Hubbard found "a valley of death in which not a blade of grass or a flower or a bunch of moss broke through the thick covering of deposited ash." The caldera itself was "the prelude to hell. Black walls, black floor, black water, deep black hole...."

Even now, there's evidence of geothermal activity. Mineral-rich warm springs near Surprise Lake bubble out of the ground at about 185 degrees. And ground temperatures near the 1931 eruption site approach 175 degrees.

But the utter blackness and destruction that Hubbard encountered have, in six decades' time, been replaced by a wide array of plant and animal life. Already, nearly 500 species of plants have repopulated the caldera, including some 200 to 300 species of mosses and lichens, and the National Park Service reports that Aniakchak has "one of the more vivid examples of terrestrial plant and animal succession found on the Alaska Peninsula."

Lichens were the first to recolonize the bare rock, gaining "tentative toeholds on barren cliffs and lava flows." During a period of years, mosses joined the lichens and slowly they created a soil hospitable to other flora. Now there's a beltlike display of plants, nearly all of which hug the ground because of Aniakchak's persistent winds. Included in the regrowth are bright meadows of wildflowers: Among the most plentiful are Kamchatka rhododendron, lupine, fireweed, arctic poppy and bluebells or mountain harebells.

Even Aniakchak's 1931 eruption site has been "transformed into a place of amazing plant diversity," says Linda Hasselbach, a Park Service employee who is studying the crater's botanical diversity for her master's thesis. "We've found several species near the center of the 1931 eruption that we haven't seen anywhere else in the caldera."

Were Aniakchak located in the Lower 48, the caldera's spectacular features would almost certainly attract hordes of visitors. Its vulcanian-crafted landscape offers diverse, breathtaking scenery. Its windswept plains, volcanic cones and lava fields afford excellent hiking, climbing and exploring. And hikers don't have to fight their way through dense alder thickets or mucky bogs to get where they're going.

But Aniakchak's remoteness, combined with high travel costs and frequently stormy weather, has kept it largely hidden from public view. The most people Miller has seen in his many trips to the caldera is 11, and they were all volcanologists making a short tour.

The caldera's visitor season is short. July and August are the preferred months to explore; by then, most of the past winter's snowfall has melted off, though the caldera's southeastern corner remains covered by glacial ice and snow year-round. In midsummer, the crater's floor is carpeted

LEFT: The caldera provides habitat for about 25 mammal species including brown bear, caribou, wolverine, porcupine, weasel, red fox, moose, an occasional wolf and some 40 species of raptors, shorebirds and songbirds. (Bill Sherwonit)

LOWER LEFT: More than 70 species of wildflowers have been identified in Aniakchak caldera, including these Kamchatka rhododendrons and bluebells or mountain harebells. (Bill Sherwonit)

with blossoms, and daytime temperatures routinely reach into the 50s and 60s, with nighttime lows in the 40s. During summer 1993, temperatures between June 21 and August 27 ranged from a high of 77 to a low of 33.

Even in summer, however, the weather can turn nasty.

Because of its topography and location, the caldera creates its own microclimate. Park staff warn that the crater's interior is subject to violent windstorms and heavy rains even when the weather outside is relatively calm. But there are also times when Pacific Ocean-generated winds called southeasters come up and over the crater walls, then whip across its floor.

Midsummer campers have had their tents ripped apart by 100-mph gales, and high winds may stir up ash clouds to 6,000 feet high. Says Miller, "Trying to walk through that is like walking through a desert sandstorm. Bad news."

And there are no camping sites

that offer complete security from the caldera's storms.

Miller, who's helped to rescue his share of campers from Aniakchak, recalls one adventurer who stayed in the caldera for several weeks in 1973. Geologists periodically flying into Aniakchak would check on the man and "each time he'd be in a little worse shape. Well, the last time we checked him, this was about three weeks later, everything was flattened and soaking wet. The guy was beat up mentally; he wanted to get out of there real bad."

Park Service researchers endured four major storms during a 9-week stay in 1993, with each storm averaging about a day and a half in length. One August storm brought winds of more than 70 mph and 3 inches of rain. Mountaineering tents built to withstand extreme weather were "just shredded by the winds," Hasselbach says. "The winds ripped several tent flies apart and we lost a couple of sets of poles," which broke from the

stress. Wind-blown ash and sand also penetrated tent zippers, ruining those as well.

"It was frightening, but wonderful, to experience the caldera's different moods," Hasselbach says.

The combination of high winds, rain and low cloud ceilings may also cause substantial delays both getting into and out of the caldera. During her 1993 sojourn, Hasselbach figured the caldera was accessible by air only 37 of 61 days, or 60 percent of the time.

As former Aniakchak Resource Manager David Mansky once put it, "Aniakchak is a grand place, but you have to be ready to deal with it on its own terms. Be prepared for the worst."

The only realistic ways of reaching the crater in summer are by air or foot — and hiking isn't

recommended. More than 15 miles of brush, marsh and wet tundra separate Aniakchak caldera from the nearest settlement at Port Heiden.

"It isn't impossible; a few people have walked in and out," Mansky says. "But it's very, very difficult."

Adds Miller, "You can do it in a day if the weather isn't bad. But the first few miles out of Port Heiden can be sloppy, miserable going."

Travel by air is just slightly less intimidating. There are no airstrips in or near the caldera so planes must land on Surprise Lake or one of the volcanic ash fields, no easy task when dealing with high winds, low ceilings or both. Just a few commercial pilots are willing and able to conduct business within the caldera.

Then there's the expense. The bush-pilot services that fly into Aniakchak operate out of King Salmon, 150 miles north. Per-person costs can run several hundred dollars, the exact amount depending on the party size and amount of equipment to be hauled.

Beyond the caldera, Aniakchak National Monument and Preserve is primarily used by whitewater river runners and big-game trophy hunters seeking brown bears or moose in the monument's preserve. And Aniakchak's barely explored coastline offers excellent wildlife-viewing and kayaking.

The National Park Service is the best source of information on Aniakchak. Contact Aniakchak National Monument and Preserve, P.O. Box 7, King Salmon, Alaska 99613, or call (907) 246 3305.

Geologic evidence suggests that half of the caldera's bottom was once covered by water several hundred feet deep, but volcanologist Tom Miller says the floor was never completely submerged, like Crater Lake, because a portion of the rim had eroded away, creating a notch, shown here, that drains water from the caldera. Known as The Gates, that notch allows the Aniakchak River to escape from the caldera and flow to the ocean. (Bill Sherwonit)

Where Alaska salmon spawn by the millions, bears are sure to follow. And the Alaska Peninsula, particularly in the north, supports some extraordinary concentrations of brown bears. "There are about 2,000 bears in the Katmai area alone," says Richard Sellers, of the Alaska Department of Fish and Game in King Salmon. "The highest density of bears ever found in the world was on the coast of Katmai, which we surveyed in 1990. We found one bear per 0.7 square miles. That's right along the coast where there is really abundant food." There may be as many as 6,000 brown bears throughout the Alaska Peninsula and Unimak Island.

Bears grow to unusual size on the peninsula, too, as large as the giant bears of Kodiak Island, across Shelikof Strait. In the spring, "when they're thin," Sellers notes, an adult, female brown bear may weigh 400 to 500 pounds. An average adult male may post a lean spring weight of 800 to 900 pounds.

The McNeil River State Game Sanctuary, immediately north of Katmai National Park, offers unusual opportunities to view brown bears as they fish for salmon. South of Katmai, Becharof Lake also supports large numbers of brown bears. The Becharof bears have the unusual habit of denning on islands within the lake. Around Ugashik Lakes, large numbers of bears feast on salmon during July and August, as they do around Black and Chignik lakes on the peninsula's Pacific side.

Bears roam the volcanic ash and lava flows on the floor of Aniakchak caldera. Father Bernard Hubbard, the Jesuit "Glacier Priest" and geologist, visited Aniakchak both before and after its 1931 eruption. In popular books, lectures and magazine articles, Father Hubbard regaled his audience with wondrous tales of Alaska. In Aniakchak, he reported muddy depressions dug into steaming volcanic vents, lined with tufts of bear fur. He speculated that bears use the fumaroles as "natural Turkish baths."

Caribou range across the Alaska Peninsula in two distinct herds. The northern herd, 16,000 to 20,000 strong, ranges from Port Moller north to the Naknek River. In recent

LEFT: One of the most prominent landmarks along the Pacific side of the Alaska Peninsula is Castle Cape, about nine miles southeast of Chignik. The cape is made up generally of non-marine and nearshore Late Cretaceous sediments about 65 million to 75 million years old. There are some deeper marine sediments toward the bottom of the cape. (George Matz)

BELOW: Izembek National Wildlife Refuge, initially designated a range, was established in 1960 in part to preserve its famed eelgrass beds, favored staging habitat each fall for virtually the world's population of black brant, a small goose. (Harry M. Walker)

ABOVE: Natalie Lind, 3, is from Chignik Lake. She is the daughter of Rona and Donnie Oscar Lind and was 2 when this photo was taken. (Jeff Caven)

ABOVE RIGHT: Calamagrostis, among the most common vegetation in the Ugashik marshlands, frames this view of the Bristol Bay lowlands looking southeast toward the Alaska-Aleutian Range. The Ugashik lowlands are well-known as a staging area for cackling Canada geese, a western Alaska species whose population crashed in the 1980s but has recovered somewhat. (Karen S. Rollinger)

years, the animals have wintered as far north as the south shore of Lake Iliamna.

The smaller southern herd ranges from Port Moller south to the peninsula's tip. Caribou on Unimak Island apparently cross Isanotski Strait to reach the mainland and are considered part of the southern peninsula herd. The southern herd as a whole has dramatically declined in the last decade. Overpopulation may have depleted lichen and other food sources and triggered the decline. The population peaked at about 10,000, in 1983. The southern herd now numbers about 2,000 caribou, including some 300 on Unimak Island. In 1993, the herd was closed to hunting, to encourage its recovery.

The moose population of the Alaska Peninsula is probably 5,000 to 6,000, according to Richard Sellers, "in the same range as bears." Moose are limited to the more wooded and brushy parts of the northern peninsula. There are virtually none south of Port Moller, where the vegetation is low and extensive stands of willow are scarce.

Wolves, on the other hand, range throughout the peninsula and as far south as Unimak Island. Sellers estimates 200 to 250 wolves inhabit the region and about 50 are taken each year by hunters and trappers. The elusive creatures have been little studied, however. Poor winter snow conditions make them hard to track.

The peninsula's land mammals are spectacular, but the region's birds and marine wildlife are an equal treasure. The rugged fiords of the Pacific resound with seabird calls. Offshore, more than 700 islands, islets and rocks fall within the Alaska Peninsula Unit of the statewide Alaska Maritime National Wildlife Refuge. Two areas of offshore water offer further refuge to marine mammals. Harbor seals occur on both sides of the peninsula, but they are in decline among some of the Pacific islands. Sea otters, once hunted to near extinction, have recolonized

many areas. Today, Steller sea lions are the center of concern. Their numbers have plummeted 80 percent during the last 30 years. They were listed as a threatened species in 1990 and may soon be classified as endangered. The cause of the sea lion crisis is not clear, but some researchers blame overfishing of pollock and other fish in a particular size range on which sea lions feed.

Seabirds by the millions use the cliffs and rubble-strewn slopes of the maritime refuge. The Shumagin, Pavlov and Semidi islands host large and diverse bird colonies. Horned and tufted puffins nest widely in the refuge. As members of the alcid family, they use their wings to "fly" while diving underwater. Murres are the deepest diving of all alcids and they can reach depths of 300 feet. They fill an ecological niche in the northern hemisphere similar to that filled by deep-diving penguins in the south. Both thick-billed and common murres nest on the cliffs of the maritime refuge. Murrelets, kittiwakes, auklets, guillemots and storm-petrels share the refuge as well.

Foxes, ground squirrels and rats are a serious problem on some islands in the region. Introduced by humans, they prey on the eggs and young of seabirds that evolved on islands without natural land predators. Foxes were farmed on more than 450 Alaska islands, first by Russians and later by Americans. Rats were inadvertently introduced from ships by fox farmers and others, including many military ships during World War II.

Ed Bailey is a U.S. Fish and Wildlife biologist with the Alaska Maritime refuge. Most refuge islands are free of rats, Bailey says, but he worries that shipwrecks could introduce them. "Compared to an oil spill, a rat spill is permanent and far more devastating," Bailey says. "Introduced species have caused more extinctions of birds on islands than anything else."

During his 25 years in the islands, Bailey has sometimes run across bigger predators: bears. They swim to some islands and feast on eggs and hatchlings, though they can't reach cliff-nesters and don't visit long. "I've actually seen them when I've been island-hopping in an inflatable (boat)," Bailey says. "I've slowed down and followed them for a while from a distance so as not to disturb them, and they just keep chugging along."

On Sutwik Island, he once fired a shotgun to keep a brown bear out of his tent. Both survived the encounter but Bailey marvels at how the bear got to the island. "It's undoubtedly a long swim," he observes. Sutwik is 14 miles off the peninsula. During summer 1993, a bear sparked concern when it turned up in Sand Point.

For the adventurous, the wildlife and scenery of the Alaska Peninsula are more accessible today than ever. In the north,

McNeil River State Game Sanctuary attracts bear lovers the world over. Bears abound as well at Brooks Falls and elsewhere within Katmai National Park and Preserve. The area was originally set aside for scientific study after Katmai's 1912 eruption, a blast that was heard 600 miles away and sent ash and debris coursing for 14 miles down a valley. The hot deposit transformed the valley into a plain as much as two-and-one-half miles wide. Steam vents and fumaroles too numerous to count

Stonewall Place at the end of the Alaska Peninsula on Isanotski Strait, is about two and one-half miles from the community of False Pass on Unimak Island. Presently owned by Buck and Shelly Laukitis, the homestead dates back many years; the previous owner, Chuck Martinson, scavenged items and built many of the systems to maintain the homestead, which has electricity supplied by a small hydro-electric system and a productive greenhouse. The greenhouse (left) and workshop are shown here. (Frederic H. Wilson/USGS)

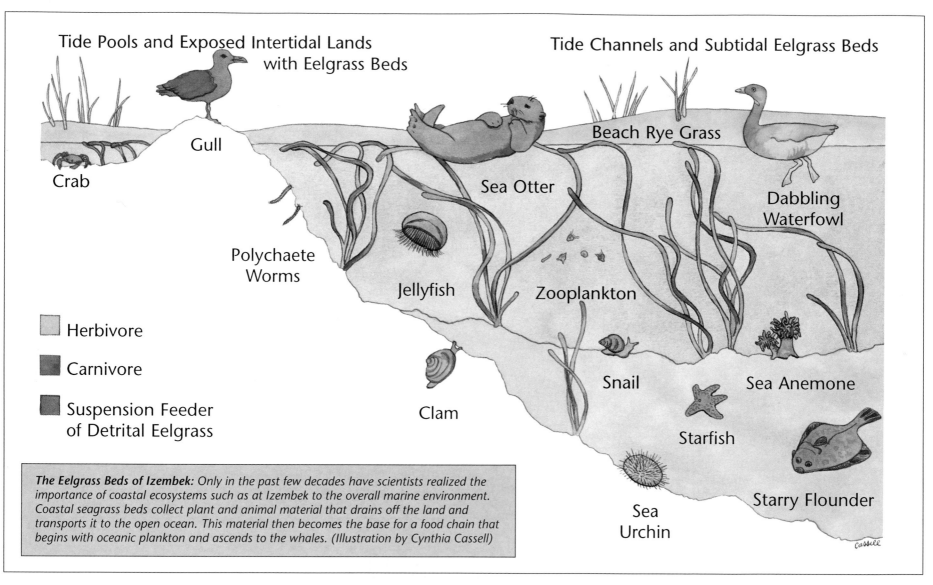

Tide Pools and Exposed Intertidal Lands with Eelgrass Beds

Tide Channels and Subtidal Eelgrass Beds

Gull

Crab

Sea Otter

Beach Rye Grass

Dabbling Waterfowl

Polychaete Worms

Jellyfish

Zooplankton

Herbivore

Carnivore

Suspension Feeder of Detrital Eelgrass

Snail

Sea Anemone

Clam

Starfish

Sea Urchin

Starry Flounder

The Eelgrass Beds of Izembek: Only in the past few decades have scientists realized the importance of coastal ecosystems such as at Izembek to the overall marine environment. Coastal seagrass beds collect plant and animal material that drains off the land and transports it to the open ocean. This material then becomes the base for a food chain that begins with oceanic plankton and ascends to the whales. (Illustration by Cynthia Cassell)

gave rise to the name the Valley of 10,000 Smokes. The valley has cooled since then but some fumaroles still issue steam. Hiking is a challenge. Trails skirt cliffs eroded deeply into deposits of tan ash hundreds of feet thick in places. The almost lunar landscape is framed by distant vistas of glaciered peaks.

More volcanic landscapes await visitors south of Katmai, in Becharof National Wildlife Refuge. The heart of the refuge is Becharof Lake, second in size in Alaska only to Lake Iliamna. Becharof spawns a million salmon a year and attracts bears, waterfowl, moose and caribou. Near the lake's southern shore are the Ukinrek Maars, a pair of explosion craters formed in 1977. Rising magma met groundwater and touched off steam explosions which rocketed steam and ash three miles skyward. Nearby, the Gas Rocks vent carbon dioxide from rock fractures linked to the maars.

On the coast of the Becharof refuge, Puale Bay is famous for harbor seals, sea lions and seabirds. The bay was fouled in 1989 by oil from the *Exxon Valdez*, aground 400 miles away. Long-term effects of the oil on Puale Bay are still under study.

South of Becharof, the Ugashik Lakes are noted for ancient archaeological sites as well as for fishing. Salteries and canneries operated for years in Ugashik village and in Pilot Point, on Ugashik Bay. Today, the mostly Aleut villagers rely on commercial fishing for income as well as on subsistence hunting, fishing and trapping.

Aniakchak National Monument and Preserve lies in the remote, central peninsula. Native hunters must have penetrated the crater, but nearby villagers professed no knowledge of the volcano prior to its "discovery" by U.S. Geological Survey scientists, in 1922. Even today, the few who visit Aniakchak brave isolation, rugged conditions and violent weather. Their reward is a volcanic wonderland of ash and lava flows, cinder cones, maars and Surprise Lake.

South of Aniakchak, the Pacific coast lies largely within the Alaska Peninsula wildlife refuge. It is a realm of foggy fiords, steep cliffs and broad beaches. Castle Cape offers magnificent scenery as do the volcanoes of the Alaska-Aleutian Range. Ice-mantled Mount Veniaminov, 30 miles wide at the base, is a nationally designated natural landmark. Near its foot is Perryville settled in 1912 by Natives who fled Katmai's eruption.

Southwest of Veniaminov, the embayment of Port Moller nearly severs the peninsula. Beyond are the southern peninsula and islands of Aleut country, a rich seascape often

obscured by clouds and storms. To the east are the Shumagin Islands, where Sand Point offers access to maritime treasures. On the southern peninsula, King Cove is a regional fishing center. Northeast of King Cove some 30 miles is 8,260-foot Pavlov Volcano, which erupts on average every six or seven years.

Finally, 40 miles from the peninsula's southwestern tip is Cold Bay. The town of Cold Bay is the gateway to the wildlife refuge surrounding Izembek Lagoon. Hundreds of thousands of waterfowl seasonally feast on eelgrass, a wetland plant rich in nutrients which abounds in the lagoon. More than 140 species of birds use the refuge. Harbor seals, sea otters, sea lions and occasionally walrus visit the refuge. Thousands of gray, killer and

Grant Point overlooks the immense eelgrass beds of Izembek lagoon. Eelgrass grows in dense concentrations, providing a stable, protected habitat for marine invertebrates and fish and foraging habitat for glaucous-winged gulls during low tide. (John Sarvis)

minke whales migrate offshore. The lagoon is one of four wetlands in the United States of recognized international importance.

Izembek and Cold Bay exemplify much of what makes the Alaska Peninsula special. The land is harsh and, although the rare, good days are tempting, it is not the weather that draws people here. For millennia, humans in this place have been sustained and nourished, body and soul, by the wildlife and the sea.

Communities of the Alaska Peninsula

The Shumagins and Sand Point

Largest of the communities within the Alaska Peninsula region is Sand Point, population 1,074, on the northwestern coast of Popof Island in the Shumagin group. Sand Point is 571 air miles southwest of Anchorage, and 87 miles west of the air hub at Cold Bay.

The history of the Shumagins parallels that of most other areas of the region. Numerous settlements including a Russian post at Red Cove on Popof were scattered throughout the islands during Russian colonial times. Codfishing and hardrock mining drew settlers to Unga, on Unga Island, which for a half century or so was the islands' dominant community. As mining and codfishing died out, Unga dwindled to a virtual ghost town and Sand Point began slow, steady growth to its current preeminent position.

Fifteen main and numerous smaller islands comprise the volcanic Shumagin group, which was once covered by a Pleistocene ice cap. Scouring and grinding of the ice fashioned a rugged landscape; later weathering smoothed some of the ruggedness, especially on Popof, but the convoluted coastline remained. This coastline and the islands' location on the route to fishing grounds for Pacific cod in Russia's Okhotsk Sea encouraged the first western commercial enterprise in the islands. In 1874 Thomas W. McCollam established a codfishing station at Pirate Cove on Popof's north coast to fish local cod stocks.

In 1887 a San Francisco company Lynde & Hough, known throughout the Pacific for its various marine-oriented enterprises including "Okhotsk Sea Cod Liver Oil," opened a supply station for the codfishery at a site the federal government had named Sand Point. Shortly, the station expanded to include a trading post and buying station for salmon. A year later, Andrew Grosvold used some of the $100,000 he had received from a successful gold claim at Nome to purchase fox farms in the area. The first families at Sand Point worked mostly for Grosvold or on dories for the codfishery.

By 1900 Sand Point counted 16 residents, mostly fishermen from Scandinavia or fur farmers raising silver and blue foxes. 1904 introduced a new element in the settlement's economy when gold was discovered on local beaches.

Unga Island already supported a handful of hardrock mines, offshoots of an original discovery in 1884 by George C. King. By 1894 several mines yielded gold and silver, including the Apollo Mine, which produced gold from that year to 1908. A resurgence in gold mining interest led Alaska Apollo Gold Mines Ltd. of Phoenix to reassess their properties on Unga from 1981 to 1987 with an eye toward reopening the mines.

Headquarters for the Aleutians East Borough, Sand Point began along the northeast shore of Humboldt Harbor. As the settlement grew, it spread over low hills between Humboldt Slough and Mud Bay. More recent additions cluster around the school out toward East Head. (Alissa Crandall)

Shumagin Islands

(Map by Kathy Doogan)

SCALE OF MILES
5   10   15

Karpa I.

UNGA STRAIT

KOROVIN ISLAND

Zachary Bay

KOROVIN STRAIT

GORMAN STRAIT

Andronica I.

Sand Point
POPOF ISLAND

POPOF STRAIT

WEST NAGAI STRAIT

Castle Rock

UNGA ISLAND

Porpoise Harbor

Northeast Bight

Unga

Delarof Harbor

Sanborn Harbor

Peninsula I.

Flying Eagle Harbor

Acheredin Bay

Eagle Harbor

Spectacle I.

BIG KONIUJI ISLAND

Hall I.

Herendeen I.

Falmouth Harbor

NAGAI ISLAND

EAST NAGAI STRAIT

Bendel I.

Atkins I.

John I.

Turner I.

KONIUJI STRAIT

LITTLE KONIUJI ISLAND

Northeast Harbor

TWELVE FATHOM STRAIT

Near I.

PACIFIC OCEAN

SIMEONOF ISLAND

BIRD ISLAND

OTTER STRAIT

CHERNABURA ISLAND

55°30'

55°00'

160°30'   160°00'   159°30'

As of late 1993, however, they remain idle.

Even earlier, in 1840, coal was mined at Coal Harbor on Unga in what was likely the first coal mining in the region. Americans resurrected the business in 1882 when they shipped about 700 tons to San Francisco, and sold smaller amounts to steamers working in the sea otter industry. By 1908 though, coal mining had dwindled to one mine.

By the 1930s, mining had quieted, the fur industry had collapsed, and fish processing stepped in to fill the gap. Fishing and fish processing remain Sand Point's economic foundation.

In 1931, Alaska Pacific Salmon Co. opened a salmon cannery on Humboldt Harbor, two miles from Sand Point; three decades later New England Fish Co. (NEFCO) converted the facility to a fish buying station. In 1980 the plant was partially burned; NEFCO sold what remained to Ocean Beauty Seafoods, then a subsidiary of Sealaska Regional Corp., the Alaska Native regional corporation for Southeast. A subsequent owner filed for bankruptcy, and local fishermen, known as the Gang of Five, bought the property.

In 1947 Aleutian Cold Storage took over Andrew Grosvold's holdings and began processing halibut the next year. Wakefield Fisheries leased part of the facility and converted it to handle king crab. Their company grew with the booming king crab industry, but just when Wakefield took over the entire plant in 1966, the industry began a steady and almost fatal decline. Sand Point had prospered with the king crab boom, and the diminished harvest temporarily halted the town's growth. To survive the economic downturn, Wakefield diversified into Tanner crab and shrimp, a pattern continued by a succession of owners until the facility was once again in the hands of Aleutian Cold Storage in 1981.

In 1986, the present owners, Trident Seafoods, took over and as of late 1993 this facility was the only fish processing plant at Sand Point. Peter Pan Seafoods has tenders and operates a fish buying station here, and they used to run a cannery at Squaw Harbor on Unga Island, but currently Peter Pan ferries all its fish to King Cove for processing.

Trident hires mostly labor from outside Alaska to serve a fleet that concentrates on salmon but goes after groundfish during salmon fishing closures. With continued price declines in the salmon industry, there is speculation that processors may boost groundfish production. In 1990, 36 million pounds of Pacific cod were processed here, in addition to smaller amounts of halibut, sablefish (black cod) and miscellaneous other groundfish. Trident also processes pollock, and the plant's employment varies from 30 during the offseason to as many as 600.

Sand Point's small boat harbor is sheltered behind a breakwater at the mouth of

Humboldt Slough. It has permanent slips for 148 vessels, 60 feet or smaller; it also has transit moorage for the temporary fleet up from Seattle for the cape fisheries [see page 69] and for the draggers and catcher boats in from the Bering Sea for the holidays. Harbormaster Bobby Galovin, in his 60s and a lifelong resident of the Shumagins, decries what he sees as the current state of over-regulation in the fishing industry. "In the '70s, we could almost fish 365 days a year; now the local fleet fishes salmon and gray cod [Pacific cod] and the opening three times a year for halibut." And what do the fishermen do when they are not out fishing? Galovin says they repair their boats, change their gear for the upcoming season and "sit around the harbor talking about the good ole days."

Although fishing has played the greatest role in Sand Point's history, many of the town's facilities were built during World War II when Sand Point was a station for minor repairs and for refueling of amphibious aircraft patrolling the Aleutians. The military's legacy was the airfield and some of the buildings.

Today Sand Point's growth has led to a stable population and an economy far more diversified than that of many Bush communities. Gale Daniels, Finance Director for the City of Sand Point, counted at least 70 businesses in Sand Point from basic services such as utilities to marine and auto repair to traditional commercial enterprises. There is a hotel, several eating places, but no bank. The grocery store will cash checks, but cash becomes a bit scarce in winter, says Daniels. The town doesn't have a doctor, but a nurse practitioner staffs the clinic, and a dentist and hygienist fly in regularly for appointments. The town's fuel and gasoline come from Trident. Daniels laments the lack of recreational facilities for young people. There is no bowling alley, no theater, no video

TOP RIGHT: For many years the preeminent community in the Shumagins, Unga flourished on the southeast corner of Unga Island. The town's economy was based on mining, government services and fishing. In an 1897 government memorandum about the controversy over moving the Customs House from Sand Point to Unga, a Col. Tingle remarked, "Unga is an old town with considerable population. It is in the direct mail route and has a post office, stores, and a gold mine which employs 150 men. Unga is an important place, so far as business is concerned." (Anchorage Museum of History and Art, Photo No. B85.28.12)

LOWER RIGHT: In the same government memorandum, Col. Tingle was not so complimentary about Sand Point. "Sand Point is the cod-fishing station of Lynde & Hough, the sole occupants of the place. It was once the rendezvous of the poaching fleet, when pelagic sealing was unlawful, but now (1896)...the sealing vessels which formerly lay there put in at Unalaska, which is at the entrance to Bering Sea. No other vessels run into Sand Point now except those of Lynde & Hough, because there is no business there to attract other than their ships. That the firm should build a hotel there is a matter of surprise to [me] as no guests are coming and going to occupy the house." (P.S. Hunt, courtesy of Anchorage Museum of History and Art, Photo No. B62.I.I.1389)

arcade, but four outlets rent videos. Sand Point's Community Recreation Committee has a pool table and games, but no place to put them, says Daniels. However, the school gym and swimming pool are open to the public, as is the school library.

As with any community far from large commercial centers, Sand Point adapts to its distance. Christmas trees, for instance, are ordered from Seattle. Artificial trees or native alders make suitable substitutes. Decorated cakes now come from cake mixes or baked-from-scratch kitchen skills; in earlier times

fancy cakes were ordered from Seward, about 550 miles to the northeast, for shipment by boat.

Nowadays, the state ferry calls at Sand Point during its summer runs down the Alaska Peninsula, and people plan around the ferry if they want to move vehicles or heavy equipment says Carol Smith, longtime resident of Sand Point who has moved to Anchorage. Most travelers, though, come and go by air, using the town's recently completed 4,000-foot runway. Late 1993 round-trip airfares between Sand Point and Anchorage were $856 on Reeve Aleutian Airways.

Subsistence fare complements store-bought supplies for Sand Pointers. Residents sport fish for salmon, halibut, Dolly Varden and trout; they hunt ptarmigan, and moose and bear on the mainland, and caribou if there is an opening. In 1993 the Shumagin Corp. offered a bison hunt on corporation land. Egg-gatherers collect gull eggs each spring, and beachcombers gather ribbon kelp in spring, and butter clams and sea urchins. They also pry chitons, locally known as bidarkies, from the rocks. These mollusks are soaked in fresh water and eaten raw or cooked. Berry-pickers look for salmonberries, mossberries, and blueberries if they can find them, in late July and August.

BELOW: Until the past few years, Peter Pan Seafoods operated this cannery built decades ago at Squaw Harbor, on Unga Island across Popof Strait from Sand Point. The cannery has since closed and Peter Pan transports its fish to King Cove for processing. As of late 1993 the Trident Seafoods plant at Sand Point was the only shore-based fish processing facility operating in the Shumagins. (Frederic H. Wilson/USGS)

RIGHT: Sand Point residents come and go mostly by plane. For those with more time or vehicles and heavy equipment to move, the state ferry Tustumena, *shown here docked at Sand Point, provides alternative transportation. (Steve McCutcheon)*

Sand Point's economy has had its ups and downs, mostly because of vagaries in the fishing industry. But generally the town's young people have remained in the community to raise their families. This stability is also reflected in the community's school system with its 148 students. Sand Point schoolchildren have a reputation for staying in school and continuing on to higher education. Teachers, adults in the community and economic times have convinced them of the need to do more than just depend on fishing, according to school district employee, Edi Hodges, 50. She continues, "Former students have become teachers and come back to Sand Point to teach. This shows [current] students that they can live in Sand Point and not be fishermen." Delores Stokes, a Sand Point native and executive secretary for the Aleutians East School District, puts it another way. Students stay in school, she says, because there is "not much else to do, no jobs, fishing is not

lucrative. Fishing is just not panning out, and you can't get into the military without a diploma." In school the students get to travel, participate in sports and acquire a good education. Among their requirements is a class in living skills where they learn about human relationships. Stokes elaborates: "Human relationships are handled well in Sand Point. We are not really as isolated as people might think. Our students travel a lot. Sand Point is an integrated community; it used to be mostly [Alaskan] Native but no longer. People are open, genuine." Stokes' point is that Sand Point, despite its location, is much like many other small towns in the United States. "We have pizza, Chinese food, a cafe by the harbor." And to counteract any impression that Sand Point is cloaked in heavy winter, Stokes says that when people from Outside write for information on the town, they are told that "we don't use down [clothing] for ice and snow, we use boots for dust and mud." ■

Growing Up in Unga

By Bob King

Editor's note: *Hubert McCallum is one of the true old-timers of the Shumagins, and Bob King, an announcer for public radio station KDLF in Dillingham and a freelance writer, offers this account of Hubert's recollections of his days in the islands off Alaska Peninsula's southern coast.*

"From the time that I was old enough to remember I've been traveling on the water. When I was 5 years old, my step-grandfather, William "Billy" Peters, took our family out on his boat. Standing beside him at the wheel, he'd be puffing his pipe and that old one-lung gas engine would be belching smoke. That combination of tobacco smoke and gas engine smoke smelled pretty good to me."

The memories come easily to Hubert McCallum on a stormy day, when it is too harsh to work outside. He sips coffee at his home in Sand Point, waiting for the weather to subside so he can work on his 58-foot seiner, the *Patricia Ann*.

Hubert was born in the Shumagin Island community of Unga. Nearly abandoned now, Unga has a long and rich history. Russian explorers noted the presence of an Aleut community here, called Ougnagok, as early as 1833. Attracted by the shallow, protected waters of Delarof Bay, the Lynde & Hough Co. of San

LEFT: Hubert McCallum, right, gathers with World War II Navy buddies from Madison, Wis., on the afterdeck of the Patricia Ann. (Courtesy of Hubert McCallum)

LOWER LEFT: He was 2, in 1922, says Hubert McCallum, when his family moved into the house in the foreground with the two-window dormer. They had moved from the U.S. Marshal's house. His dad served as marshal at Unga from 1918 to 1922. According to Hubert, the only animal using Unga as a home now is an old horse (shown at center) that takes shelter in the basement of the old general store. (Hubert McCallum)

Francisco established a codfishing station here in 1888. Then called Ounga, the name was shortened to Unga five years later.

In 1891, prospectors discovered a rich vein of gold-bearing quartz three miles from Unga. Through 1905, the Apollo Mine produced more than $2 million worth of gold. The vein, however, ran out in 1912. Production fell and the mine sputtered to a close 10 years later.

A second disaster hit Unga at about the same time. Increased demand for seafood products during World War I attracted many fishermen to the Shumagin cod banks. Catches soared during the war but the stocks collapsed immediately afterward.

A new fishery was emerging at the same time, however. Pacific

American Fisheries built the first salmon cannery at King Cove on the mainland near Cold Bay in 1911. Several other canneries were built elsewhere in the region, including Squaw Harbor on Unga Island in 1920, but Unga itself was ignored. Delarof Bay, which provided great protection for the small cod dories, was just too shallow for the larger salmon boats.

The decline of gold and cod and the rising importance of salmon spelled a slow end for Unga. While many residents took seasonal jobs at the nearby Squaw Harbor cannery, Unga's population dropped from a peak of 313 in 1920 to 150 10 years later.

LEFT: Hubert McCallum's seiner, the Patricia Ann, *is one of the last built by the Harold Hansen Boat Co. in Seattle. This family-owned boat building company and repair yard began production about the 1940s. The company still exists, although they have dropped Harold's name. The Hansen Boat Co. is now located in Marysville, Wash., and Hubert says Hansen-built boats are the "best boats on the Pacific coast." (Rob Stapleton, courtesy of Hubert McCallum)*

ABOVE: Hubert McCallum, born Nov. 27, 1920, at Unga, relaxes in his easy chair on the bridge of the Patricia Ann. *(Courtesy of Hubert McCallum)*

Many residents moved to nearby Sand Point, another cod station established in 1887. Sand Point offered a better harbor for deep draught vessels. Residents of other abandoned cod stations at Sanak and Korovin also moved here. Construction of a military base during World War II helped establish Sand Point as the population center of the Shumagins.

Its economic base gone; its population dwindling, Unga slowly lapsed into obscurity. The Unga post office was officially closed in 1958.

Hubert McCallum was born in 1920, the son of a Scottish-Irish immigrant who served as the U.S. marshal at Unga. His mother was the daughter of a Danish codfisherman and his wife of Aleut-Russian descent.

Although Unga is perhaps one of the most remote communities in Alaska, McCallum has fond memories of growing up here.

"We had a shallow bay and when the tide would go out, well, you would go out there and wade up to your knees and catch Dungeness crab and dig a sack full of clams," McCallum recalled. "Then we had the old mine to go up and visit. We had an agate beach, we had an ocean beach. We had mountains to climb. There was a cave out there we used to go down into and explore. We had the old Kelly's Rock fish station, about a 45 minute hike, and ptarmigan to hunt, several trout fishing streams, ice skating ponds, slopes where we skied and slid on toboggans. Just name it and it seems like we had it.

"I was raised on the water. When we were little kids and it got rough in that open harbor we'd steal dories and skiffs and go out and ride the surf. That was a highlight to get out there and ride the breakers in an open skiff. The first time I went out with my uncle I was 5 or 6 years old. I sat in the stern until I got old enough to handle an oar."

In his teens, McCallum began to work for the salmon cannery at Squaw Harbor. "I got my first job out on the fish traps. Pacific American Fisheries had traps at Pinnacle and Kelly's Rock and Cape Swedania in those days. I worked on a pile driver for two years and then on a rigging scow. The pile driver would drive the piling and the riggers would put the cross bars and planking on the trap. Then, of course, you had the web crew. It took three different crews to build the fish trap." McCallum's salary on the trap crews was a base of $65 a month plus a percentage based on the actual fish pack.

Fish traps were efficient, but despised by Alaskans who saw them as only taking jobs away from resident fishermen. Despite their objections, however, nobody said anything bad about them.

"Oh, certainly we resented the

traps but the companies were the king and you had better not say anything bad about the king or you'd find yourself without a job. You couldn't say anything derogatory about the superintendent or the company or you'd be spanked. You wouldn't get a fishing job or a job on the pile driver."

McCallum worked for the trap crews for four years when in 1936 his mother, pregnant with her fifth child, decided to move the family to Anchorage. McCallum graduated from Anchorage High School and the family continued to return to the Shumagins every fishing season until World War II erupted. McCallum enlisted in the Navy and served on a destroyer throughout most of the war. Toward the end of the conflict, however, the military called upon his experience as a fisherman to provide food for the troops. McCallum found himself in charge of a sampan in the Mariana Islands, fishing for tuna with a crew of Japanese.

After the war, McCallum attended the University of Washington under the GI bill. He studied accounting and later took on office jobs. The pay was good, he recalls, but he still missed life in the Shumagins.

"I didn't care for accounting, that's all there is to it. One of the last jobs I had was for a company that built television antenna systems. It was quite a business. We had about 10 jobs going in four different states but it was too much of a headache. I just quit one evening. I said I'm going back

to Alaska and find a fishing job. Flew back to Anchorage in one of those Constellations. The Constellation was the new thing back then."

McCallum at first fished with his brother in the Chignik area and then returned to the Shumagins, moving permanently to Sand Point in 1970. He has fished here from the same boat ever since.

"The *Patricia Ann* was the last Harold Hansen wood boat built. I had that boat built for $112,000 in 1966 and since that I have put in two increments of capital construction fund money. $226,000 twice. I might say if you look at the economy of a boat, I have one of the cheaper purse seiners. The boats that are coming out now are a million and a third or a million and a half a copy."

Now semiretired, McCallum has largely turned the *Patricia Ann* over to Hubert McCallum Jr. But he still likes to get out on the water, if only to take some of his

ABOVE: Unga may have been remote, but there was no lack of imaginative play for children growing up here. Hubert McCallum (left) recalls for his friend from Wisconsin how as a child he used to play engineer with this old donkey engine that stood on the fish dock and hoisted freight out of dories and the mail boat. (Courtesy of Hubert McCallum)

RIGHT: Wild iris, also known as blue flag, are among several wildflower species that brighten the Unga landscape. (Steve McCutcheon)

buddies from his destroyer days out on a fishing trip or to visit his old home.

"We go over to Unga once or twice during the summer when we get a break from salmon and walk through town. Most of the buildings are falling down. The house I was born in is still standing and you can kind of stumble through it on the broken down floors but in a few years there won't be anything left to see.

"The home where my wife, Dorothy, was raised is still standing. Nancy Stonington was there and did a sketch. We have a watercolor of hers looking down from a hill on Dorothy's home and the wreckage of the old codfish station and the bay. It's kind of a memento.

"One of the most enjoyable things I can do is get out aboard the boat," says McCallum. "I have friends from World War II, destroyer friends that come over. Parties of four, five or six come over here for a week or so and I take them out on the boat and fish and cruise. It's still one of the most enjoyable things I do."

Cold Bay

Cold Bay's biggest asset stretches nearly two miles across the flat, windswept tundra. It's a 10,400-foot runway, a legacy of the town's origin as a World War II military base and its current claim to fame.

Located 40 miles from the western tip of the Alaska Peninsula, Cold Bay sits on a pinch of low land between the Bering Sea and

Chuck Yates holds one of Russell Creek's renowned silver salmon. Chuck and his wife, Darlene, are on their second tour of duty in Cold Bay where Chuck manages the weather service office. (Darlene Yates)

Pacific Ocean. If sea levels rose 100 feet, the place would be swamped. But instead, Cold Bay offers a refuge to fliers of all descriptions.

Blowy, cloudy weather prevails. But only do the worst storms turn planes away. Cold Bay's lighted runway is one of the longest in the state, behind those at Eielson Air Force Base in Fairbanks and Anchorage International Airport. Pilots coming into Cold Bay can lock onto modern navigational aids for instrument landings, and a mile-long crosswind runway gives them a choice of headings. Cold Bay's facilities are, in fact, considered among the best in the universe; NASA has designated Cold Bay for emergency space shuttle landings.

Surrounding Cold Bay is Izembek National Wildlife Refuge, to some of North America's migrating waterfowl what the town's airport is to flying machines. The refuge protects Izembek Lagoon and its eelgrass beds, critical feeding and staging area for seabirds, shorebirds and waterfowl, particularly black brant. A glassed-in observatory with viewing scope at Grant Point, 10 miles by road from town, offers good vantage.

Each fall, the continent's entire brant population flocks to Izembek. They fatten on eelgrass for nonstop migration to wintering grounds as far south as Mexico. "They're over there now. It's incredible to watch thousands of geese rise in a black mass off the water," said Chick Beckley, principal of Cold Bay School, on his way to the lagoon one early November afternoon. "All those wings sound like a jet engine roar. It's humbling to watch that many birds get up and move."

Cold Bay's orientation to the sky, rather than the sea, makes it an oddity for the Alaska Peninsula.

It has a dock and harbor, but no commercial fishermen. For now, the only nets that get wet in Cold Bay belong to subsistence and sport fishermen. The Aleutians East

Borough has recently completed a $2 million expansion of the old dock to serve vessels coming into Cold Bay off the Pacific Ocean. With the dock and the airport to speed fresh fish shipments, deliveries of boat parts and crew changes, Cold Bay could become a player in the commercial fisheries.

Residents already proclaim Cold Bay the sport fishing and hunting paradise of the lower peninsula. They fish for salmon, trout and grayling in Russell Creek, halibut off the dock, and king crab in the bay. The Labor Day weekend Silver Salmon Derby, complete with a raffle for airline tickets out of town, is an annual big deal. Along with tremendous numbers of waterfowl at the lagoon, there are plenty of upland game birds such as ptarmigan. The southern peninsula caribou herd migrates through town, often congregating on the runway. Wolves, foxes and brown bears live all around. "I stepped outside one night to get something out of my truck," recalls Beckley, "and there on my porch, close enough to touch, was a bear. We see them walking through town all the time."

The pursuit of wildlife, with gun or camera, is aided by some 60 miles of old military roads around town. Few Bush communities have such a road network. A Sunday drive can last several hours without backtracking.

All this aside, everyone in Cold Bay knows why they're really here. "The only reason Cold Bay exists is because of our long runway," says businessman Rick Schlichten. It is the region's transportation hub for mail, cargo and passengers. Some of its regular users are private corporate jets and cargo carriers refueling during flights between North America and Asia. Actor Richard Gere was among recent visitors, and the Wrigley family, of chewing gum fame, usually overnights in Cold Bay en route to the Orient.

With the runway comes the town's jobs. Schlichten, for instance, manages Pavlof

Services, a branch of Reeve Aleutian Airways that owns a big chunk of the town's businesses — the restaurant, store, hotel, bar and fuel depot. Cold Bay's vintage collection of small wooden buildings is updated by a proliferation of satellite dishes picking up news and sit-coms. The city hall houses a much-used library with an extensive collection of videos, along with a public weight room.

Cold Bay's bar, the Weathered Inn, dates back to the famous cargo company Flying Tigers, which operated here after the war. More than one stranded traveler has knocked back a few cold ones at the Weathered Inn. "We've had some parties," recalls Schlichten.

False Pass

The Aleut town of False Pass, on the east end of Unimak Island, is narrowly separated from the lower Alaska Peninsula by Isanotski Strait. About 70 people live here, most of whom are commercial fishermen. Unimak Island had a dozen Aleut settlements in the mid-1800s during Russian occupation, but the community of False Pass developed in the early 1900s around a salmon cannery. Today at the old cannery site, Peter Pan Seafoods, Inc. operates a fish camp, with docks, carpentry and machine shops, and a store that stays open year-round. Peter Pan shut down the cannery lines after a 1981 fire.

False Pass is closely related through kinship, culture and economy to the peninsula, and is part of the Alaska Maritime National Wildlife Refuge. For more about False Pass, look for *ALASKA GEOGRAPHIC®*'s forthcoming, new Aleutian Islands issue, which will cover this community in greater depth. (Frederic H. Wilson/USGS)

Pavlof Services' bar, restaurant, package store and grocery store constitute the business core of downtown Cold Bay. One resident says that visitors sometimes ask where the town is when they're standing in the middle of it. (Harry M. Walker)

"Once someone shot the jukebox because they didn't like the song."

Most of Cold Bay's 150 residents are attached to state or federal government agencies. State transportation crews maintain the airport. The Federal Aviation Administration flight service station provides about 60,000 pilot weather briefings and flight plans a year. The National Weather Service issues aviation and marine forecasts. The U.S. Fish and Wildlife Service headquarters in town oversees the Izembek refuge, along with the Unimak Island unit of the Alaska Maritime National Wildlife Refuge and the Pavlof unit of the Alaska Peninsula National Wildlife Refuge.

Two decades ago, the population was nearly twice as many, before the Air Force

closed its remaining facilities and the FAA phased out some jobs. But Cold Bay is a shadow of its wartime heyday, when some 60,000 people crowded into Fort Randall.

The military built Fort Randall in 1941 at the beginning of World War II as a strategic air, army and naval base to protect Dutch Harbor, 180 miles to the west. Fort Randall's identity was disguised as a fish cannery to thwart enemy intelligence. At the time, a Navy pensioner was supposedly Cold Bay's sole inhabitant. No one seems to know what he was doing there, but the noisy construction apparently drove him away.

In June 1942, Fort Randall launched fighters and bombers against the Japanese attacking Dutch Harbor. The next year, American forces — battleships, cruisers, destroyers, escort carriers, submarines and troop transports for 10,000 soldiers — staged at Cold Bay for an amphibious assault on Japanese-occupied Attu and Kiska islands. It was the largest American force assembled since the bloody Battle of Guadalcanal, wrote

Jonathan Nielson in *Armed Forces on a Northern Front* (1988).

Cold Bay seemed a bleak outpost, a lonely group of buildings at the foot of snow-covered mountains. According to John Cloe in *The Aleutian Warriors* (1991), a marine captain on the incoming fleet wrote in his diary: "The ships look out of place in a world that belongs so little to men."

Near war's end, Cold Bay became a transfer station in America's lend-lease military air program. Destroyers, supplies and munitions came through Cold Bay for United States allies.

The Navy also conducted secret training for Russians at Cold Bay. Some 2,500 Russian marines and other soldiers in 1945 learned amphibious landings and warfare, to use in attacking Japanese bases in the Kurile Islands. Cold Bay continues today a transient community, much as it was during military years. People rotate through Cold Bay as their career demands. Many of them stay only a couple of years. "Most everybody's an outsider," muses Beckley, "so nobody's an outsider."

Izembek biologist Chris Dau and his family are some of the few Cold Bay old-timers. They've lived here about 13 years.

A few government employees are in their second residency. Chuck Yates, manager of the weather service office, and his wife, Darlene, were first here in the early 1980s. They were glad to return, said Yates, because they like to fish and they enjoy the quiet, small town atmosphere. "Everybody knows everybody else. And there's no crime. You couldn't steal anything because everybody would know who it belongs to," Yates said.

But Cold Bay may never qualify as anyone's true home. It lacks the generational continuity and cultural identity of neighboring Native villages. No one in recent times has ever stayed in Cold Bay long enough to be buried here, as far as anyone knows. It doesn't even have a cemetery. ■

King Cove

An early winter day found the King Cove harbor busy with boats. Although salmon fishing was over for another year, the huge Peter Pan cannery was gearing up for crab processing. Boats from Seattle and Kodiak docked one after another to take on crab pots, which had been stacked in outdoor storage around town since the end of last season.

King Cove and its cannery, the nation's largest, sit on a spit between steep mountains at the head of a bay off Deer Passage on the peninsula's south side. The cannery complex occupies nearly half of the 55-acre spit. Much of the rest of town is crammed into an area about the size of a big Kmart store. New homes spill off the spit onto nearby uplands.

The number of people living in King Cove fluctuates with fishing and seafood processing seasons. The 1990 federal census counted 451 permanent residents, yet the city uses a figure almost double that. The city maintains that a mid-1980s annexation of lands embracing the two newest subdivisions was not counted in the 1990 census. These annexations jump King Cove's population to 724. In addition, Peter Pan employs 100 to 450 people, mostly out-of-towners who live out their contracts in company housing. Fishermen flood town in summer, jumping the population to around 1,500. Bodies pack one of the town's popular watering holes, the Last Hook-Off with its 97-foot horseshoe-shaped bar, reputedly the longest in Alaska.

Since its origin as a cannery town early this century, King Cove has grown steadily. The town just got its first deep-water public dock, an alternative to the cannery dock for fishing boats and the state ferry during its summertime visits. A deeper outer harbor dock is in the works for 70-foot to 150-foot fishing vessels that do business in town and have little place now to moor.

On shore, a long-discussed hydroelectric project appears to be nearing reality, to replace the city's diesel-fired electrical system. Among other things, a new power plant will enable the city to light up its airport runway.

Planes headed for King Cove need all the help they can get. The town is served by regularly scheduled flights out of Cold Bay, 18 miles to the northwest, but that doesn't mean that planes regularly fly.

King Cove gets the fallout when warm North Pacific air tangles with cold air off the

Mount Dutton (4,834 feet) towers behind the Russian Orthodox church at King Cove. The Alaska Peninsula extends through Alaska's more southerly latitudes, which moderates the seasonal shifts in temperature and day length. King Cove sits about the same latitude as Ketchikan in Southeast Alaska. Winter temperatures in this part of the peninsula average in the low 20s, while normal summer temperatures hover in the high 50s and low 60s. The peninsula's climate is further influenced by ocean on both sides, a situation which brings fog, rain, storms and high winds to the land. (Dee Randolph)

is precarious, because of constantly changing and generally lousy weather against the backdrop of steep mountains.

But that didn't concern the seafarers who settled King Cove in 1911. The fishermen could sail their boats right up to the spit. The embayment offered a natural ice-free harbor with easy access to the fishing grounds. Soon after Pacific American Fisheries opened its salmon cannery, Scandinavian and other northern European fishermen arrived. Some of them married Aleut women.

Gradually Aleuts from Belkofski, Thin Point, Morzhovoi, Ikatan and False Pass came to King Cove. The men fished and the women worked in the cannery. Of all the villages, King Cove drew heaviest from Belkofski, located in the next bay east.

Belkofski had been settled around 1823 by Aleuts, including some from Sanak, under Russian direction to hunt nearby sea otter colonies. During its boom years, historians say, Belkofski was likely the most affluent Aleut village. In 1880, the village had three stores and its residents imported building materials and home furnishings from San Francisco. The Russian Orthodox Church made Belkofski its administration center for the eastern Aleutians and western Alaska Peninsula.

But decimation of the sea otter spelled the slow death of Belkofski. People began leaving the village in the summers to fish out of King Cove, work in the cannery, or hunt seals in the Pribilof Islands. Families moved away. By the 1970s, Belkofski had no store, clinic, bar or transportation. As King Cove was getting satellite television, telephones, and water and sewer, Belkofski residents still relied on gas and kerosene for heating and cooking, used outhouses and hauled water from streams. Claude Kuzakin Sr., who grew up there, said his family moved to King Cove in 1976, and the last year-round residents left the village

ABOVE: One of the largest communities on the Alaska Peninsula, King Cove, population 724, is nestled at the base of steep mountains overlooking a lagoon and cove with the same name. (Dee Randolph)

LEFT: Not much is left of the once bustling sea otter hunting center of Belkofski, east of King Cove. The last families moved from here to King Cove in the mid-1980s, and the Orthodox church, center, collapsed in 1992. (Staff)

Bering Sea. Conditions are worst during July and August, when fog and clouds hang thick about half the time. Storms moving east from the Aleutian Islands hit often and winds howl through the narrow valley. Flying into town

in the mid-1980s. The Orthodox church, a National Historical Landmark, was blown down by 100 mph winds during a November 1992 snowstorm, said Kuzakin, who was moving his fishing boat along the beach at the time. The church's trappings and icons had been taken years earlier to King Cove. A couple of homes left standing are occasionally used in summer by families from King Cove.

In the meantime, the cannery in King Cove changed ownership numerous times through the years. It burned and was rebuilt more than once. As the fisheries changed, the facility changed, expanding and retooling to process crab, salmon roe and pollock in addition to canning salmon. In 1980, the Japanese corporation Nichiro Gyogya Kaisha bought the plant from Bristol Bay Native Corp.

King Cove fishermen chase sockeye salmon all over lower peninsula waters through the summer. Depending on the size of their boat and their daring, they may fish commercially for cod or pollock in winter.

A few King Cove salmon fishermen find jobs aboard the crab boats, which after a brief stopover head on to the Bering Sea winter crab fishery around the Pribilof Islands. About 50 of these boats deliver their catch back to the Peter Pan plant. By working on the crab boats, a King Cove fisherman can make extra money toward his boat payments, an important consideration in 1993 when salmon prices hit the skids.

It also was a year rife with bickering. The King Cove fishermen participate in the controversial intercept fisheries of the lower Alaska Peninsula. "All those guys up north are hollering that we're stealing their fish all the time," explains Harold "Skinny" Bendixen one afternoon at his home. "The Bristol Bay guys are hollering about we're catching their reds. The Kuskokwim yelling we're catching their dogs. We're just the bad guys, I guess."

Since 1949, Bendixen has drift gillnetted out of King Cove, starting in June each year with the South Unimak fishery, then moving around to Port Moller. A few years ago, he sold his 36-foot boat and turned over his limited entry salmon permits to his two sons. Now he works for them. He's seen the south peninsula fisheries become increasingly regulated and controversial, particularly compared to the early years when a man's stamina was about the only thing that limited his catch.

In the off months, the fishermen in town repair and hang nets, beachcomb, tell stories, play bingo, attend an occasional polka dance and hunt. Along with salmon, families here eat locally killed waterfowl and game. Hunting caribou for food is usually a popular pastime, but caribou seasons have grown shorter in recent years and didn't open at all in 1992 or 1993. The southern peninsula herd, which ranges south of Port Moller, has dropped the past decade from 10,000 animals to a low of around 2,000. State biologists think the animals are suffering poor nutrition from inadequate forage. Bendixen wryly suggests another cause: "Those guys up in Bristol Bay must be gettin' them." ■

The core of King Cove fits snugly on a 55-acre spit. New subdivisions on nearby benchlands and linear growth around the cove have enabled the town to expand into a population and commercial center. (Matt Johnson)

Nelson Lagoon

Each spring the people of Nelson Lagoon launch their skiffs and boats, ready with their nets for the first returns of salmon. Most everyone in this small, close-knit Aleut village fishes commercially. It is family tradition.

Nelson Lagoon is located on the north side of the Alaska Peninsula. The lagoon is part of a major indentation in the coastline that forms Port Moller and Herendeen Bay. The people of Nelson Lagoon descend from Aleuts who lived throughout this region. Artifacts and ancient middens indicate that Aleuts fished and hunted sea mammals around this embayment several thousand years ago.

The modern village of Nelson Lagoon sits on a narrow sand spit that separates the like-named lagoon from the Bering Sea. The spit joins flat, marshy tundra to the south called Caribou Flats. Here salmon-rich rivers — the David and Sapsuk, locally known as the Hoodoo — flow into the lagoon. In winter, ice forms in the shallow lagoon, and tides pile up the ice 4 feet thick in places. Storm waves and winds pound the low spit from both sides, eroding feet of beach each year despite a locally built breakwater.

At the northeast end, the lagoon opens into Port Moller, which prongs off into Herendeen Bay.

In the 1820s, Russian explorers sailed into the embayment, naming Port Moller after one of their sloops. In the late 1800s, the U.S. Coast and Geodetic Survey mapped the region. By this time, local Aleuts had concentrated at Mashikh on Port Moller, around the mouth of Bear River a few miles north along the coast, and in Herendeen Bay. Russian blood flowed among some of these Natives, from unions between fur traders and Aleut women.

Salmon salteries and canneries started appearing. Capt. Herendeen built a saltery at Port Moller in 1886. A saltery went in at Nelson Lagoon in 1906, but folded a few years later. In 1915, a salmon cannery was built on Egg Island, less than a mile from the present-day village. It operated sporadically for a few years.

Scandinavian fishermen began showing up to work fish traps and drift nets. Scandinavians had been part of the codfishing fleets in Bristol Bay and the Shumagins since the 1870s. Sometime after the turn of the century, several Scandinavian fishermen, including Martin Gundersen, "Happy" Jorgenson and Fred Nelson, settled in the Nelson Lagoon area and married Native women.

This era also brought coal mining to Herendeen Bay, part of the larger Chignik field. Bituminous and some lignite coals were mined in the southeast part of the bay at Mine Harbor in 1898. Between 200 and 300 tons of coal were shipped out the next year, and the mine closed. Two attempts to further develop the mine occurred in 1898 and 1904, and at some point a railroad route was surveyed over the mountains to Balboa Bay on the Pacific side. The coal was used mostly by local canneries and steamships, markets that died when fuel oil came into use.

Sometime around the turn of the century, a group of Eskimos and at least one discouraged miner from the Seward Peninsula showed up. Charles Franz, 83, was born in Nelson Lagoon in 1910 to a Swedish miner and his Eskimo wife. Franz did not know his father and his mother died when he was 2. But old-timers told Franz that his parents were among about 100 Eskimos who migrated down the coast in a two-year trip by skin boats.

During a telephone conversation from his home in Washington state, Franz recalls growing up in Nelson Lagoon. He said he was raised by a Latvian fisherman-trapper named Julius Franz. Another trapper, Archie Turnbull, taught him reading, writing and arithmetic. As a boy, Franz roamed the area with Turnbull's big dog Friday, a Saint Bernard-Labrador mix that Franz rode like a horse.

A government source says the Eskimo immigrants and the Aleuts did not get along well, and most of the Eskimos eventually moved to the Ugashik River.

Franz recalls steam tugs pulling scows of salmon into the saltery at Nelson Lagoon. The fish was salted in large vats, then packed into barrels and loaded onto sailing schooners. The remains of a three-masted schooner trapped by ice in Nelson Lagoon can still be found.

In 1918-19, a flu epidemic ravaged the region, killing many people. Few families were untouched. In several cases, motherless children were sent away to orphanages.

The years after brought a flurry of activity. In the late teens and early 1920s, a herring

reduction plant and three salmon canneries opened around Herendeen Bay; one cannery opened at Port Moller.

A number of families lived in Herendeen Bay, even after the canneries closed. Franz, living on the south side of Nelson Lagoon, became a legislator with statehood. His priority was to get a school for his home region. Although Herendeen Bay hosted the larger community, Nelson Lagoon was the fishing center. Several families, including widow Polly Nelson and her 12 children, agreed to move to the spit and the new village of Nelson Lagoon got a school. The Charles Franz school in 1993 had about a dozen students and one teacher.

Over at Port Moller, the Pacific American Fisheries cannery closed in 1964, due to a fish shortage. It soon reopened as a fish buying station under Peter Pan Seafoods, although

some salting continued. The whole fresh fish were tendered to Peter Pan processors in False Pass and King Cove. Today, Peter Pan operates cold storage at Port Moller, employing about 130 people spring through early fall. Most of the workers are from Outside. Summer fishing adds 450 people to Nelson Lagoon's year-round population of 80 to 90.

In winter, a caretaker at the facility sells fuel to crab vessels and relays supplies between planes and boats using Peter Pan's 3,000-foot gravel airstrip and dock. The closest neighbors are an Aleut couple, about seven miles away.

For nearly 17 years, Joe Sanger worked as winter caretaker. Before taking the job, he had fished in the bay, and before that he had worked as lead mechanic on the government's White Alice communication site above the plant. This station has been inactive for years,

John Knight checks his stake setnet during early morning fishing near Nelson Lagoon. The stakes are used as vertical spacers to keep the net taut between the cork line on top and the lead line at the bottom. This method of fishing was more common in earlier times; modern equipment has made this practice obsolete. (Courtesy of Valarie Johnson)

and the towers are scheduled for demolition in 1994.

Winter in Port Moller is usually quiet, good for beachcombing, hunting, trapping, fishing and watching television, said Sanger. The plant has two satellite dishes for television reception.

One year, Sanger and a lodge owner boated across Port Moller and poured a concrete-sided bathing pool at the old hot springs, which had been worked on in the 1930s by Charles Franz and his friends. The springs get occasional use by Nelson Lagoon villagers, summer Peter Pan workers, and passing fishermen in the know. An old Aleut site near the hot springs dates back 3,500 years. An abandoned house from modern times has been ravaged by bears, Sanger said.

"You really have to watch out for bears out here," said Sanger shortly before he retired in winter 1993. He recalled two separate

The Charles J. Franz High School honors one of Nelson Lagoon's more illustrious former residents, who as a legislator at statehood in 1959 shepherded through legislation to finance a school for his home community. (Courtesy of Valarie Johnson)

incidents when 21 bears got into the Peter Pan warehouse, and nine bears trashed the mess hall.

Nelson Lagoon villagers have depended on Peter Pan for decades. Most of the village fishermen sell to Peter Pan and in return, they have access to the Peter Pan dock and facilities.

Nelson Lagoon's short gravel airstrip accommodates small planes for passengers and light supplies, but large freight shipments come by water. The village used to get heavy cargo, equipment and lumber delivered twice a year on a Bureau of Indian Affairs barge out of Seattle. The barge operated a lightering service that landed the freight on the spit. The barge service is rarely used now because rates have increased under a new operator. Now freight comes in by private cargo carrier to the Peter Pan dock, and the villagers make a sometimes rough, 30-mile water crossing to pick up the goods in their skiffs.

This may change. The village's decade-old dream for a public dock seems poised to happen. A $2 million dock and boat launch project is scheduled for construction in 1994, funded in part by the Aleutians East Borough and the Aleutian Pribilof Islands Community Development Association. This association was one of six created in southwestern Alaska to implement community development quotas for pollock and to aid business dealings between the communities and groundfish processors.

When completed, Nelson Lagoon's dock will be the only public dock between False Pass and Egegik, says borough coordinator Sharon Boyette. The leadership of Nelson Lagoon has been described as astute and able, particularly in maintaining village control over its local fishery. They look to the dock as providing another degree of autonomy. It may attract other fish buyers, giving villagers a choice of markets. Its boat ramp could allow

development of boat storage for other fishermen, perhaps leading to other businesses and much needed jobs.

Nelson Lagoon villagers fish all summer to make enough money to last the year. The local fleet consists of about two dozen drift gillnetting boats and about 45 smaller skiffs used for drift and setnetting. Families spend a good part of the winter mending nets, painting boats, repairing engines and electronic equipment; and subsistence hunting for caribou, moose, ducks and geese, fishing for halibut and crab, and gathering berries and beach foods. A few people work part-time at the school, store and village council.

Winter fun includes ice fishing, snow sledding and evening activities at the school gym. Students starting in seventh grade play basketball and volleyball against teams from Cold Bay, False Pass and Akutan. These small schools put together three-person, coed teams for weekend tournaments. "It's one of the few social outlets for the kids during the school year," says village principal Linn Clawson.

Air travel from Nelson Lagoon is expensive. Flights to Cold Bay, 80 miles away, are scheduled several days a week for about $90 a seat, one way. Air charters cost about $350 one way. From Cold Bay, round-trip fares to Anchorage run $430 to $775. Villagers travel out only occasionally, sometimes for medical care.

Nelson Lagoon's village health aide offers routine care from a tiny clinic inside the post office building. The examination room barely holds a table; thin walls afford little privacy. Patients must wait in the post office lobby, and a doctor visits once a year. The village is trying to get money to build a modern facility, but for now, villagers needing additional care see a nurse practitioner at Cold Bay's new clinic. Or they can continue on to a hospital in Anchorage or Dillingham. ∎

Paul's Wife: Justine Gundersen of Nelson Lagoon

By Bob King

Paul's wife sports a tattoo on her left forearm, a flower with a heart intertwined in its stems.

"Well, I thought I was going never to see a flower again, so I decided to get a flower so I could see it all the time. The heart, of course, is just the icing on the cake."

Justine Gundersen laughs when she recalls getting the flower tattoo. It was a last minute impulse just before she and her husband at the time moved from Seattle to Port Moller, a seemingly improbable move for then Justine Chesley.

Born in 1938 into an Italian family in New Jersey, just across the river from New York City, Justine grew up in Minnesota, was educated in Virginia and ultimately migrated to California. She traveled about the West Coast from Mexico to Seattle. Along the way she met her second husband, a newspaper writer who in 1974, seeking a sabbatical, decided to take a winter watchman's job at a cannery in Port Moller.

It was even more improbable, it seems, for her husband Frank. One winter was enough for him. Frank left. Justine and a son from her previous marriage stayed. Justine had fallen in love with the Alaska Peninsula and had met a man named Paul Gundersen.

"What was my first reaction to Port Moller? I don't know. I just thought it was so beautiful. It was

ABOVE: Justine Gundersen, 55, displays her tattoo, a reminder of one of the many improbable episodes that have spiced her journey from New Jersey to Nelson Lagoon. (Bob King)

LEFT: The late Paul Gundersen, a leader of Nelson Lagoon, has a word with his dog Ramsey Barker. (Justine Gundersen)

in the fall. It was a whole different lifestyle. Theo, my son, 12, did go a little bonkers. But there was a village across the way at Nelson Lagoon and it was either Theo going there or down (to the Lower 48) with his grandparents. And I kind of zeroed in on Paul because Paul was divorced and still had his son there and I thought, gosh, this guy would be a nice guy to have Theo stay with."

Paul Gundersen was born in Nelson Lagoon, Sept. 16, 1921. His father was a Norwegian fisherman, his mother a Russian-Aleut. She died shortly after Paul was born and he was sent to an orphanage in Dillingham. At age 8, Paul returned to Herendeen Bay where he roamed with the bears, Justine says. He even had a bear for a pet. During World War II, Paul served with Castner's Cutthroats in the Aleutians. He returned to the peninsula after the war where he fished and trapped, got married, had five children, got divorced, and met Justine, who was also just divorced. They were married in 1976. It was another improbable move on Justine's part. Paul had just undergone open heart surgery. And getting married was an alternative to going to the dentist.

"That's actually how it happened. He was such a healthy guy and the operation was so successful that I thought, well, while we're in Seattle we should have everything done, you should have your teeth done. He said, 'No, I don't want to.... I don't want any more shots.' I said, 'Well, all right, let's get married.' He said o.k., so we got married. And it has been nice ever since. It was a good relationship. We worked together."

And work they did. Paul Gundersen had emerged as the leader of Nelson Lagoon. A high-line fisherman, Paul naturally assumed a leadership role in the village council and village corporation. It was the 1970s, the decade of the Alaska Native land claims settlement, and a lot of work needed to be done.

"Paul was a great leader. He was a visionary, but conservative and stable. He directed his people well. Nothing really ruffled him. Why we had a relationship I'll never know because I'm a short-tempered, erratic Italian. But we worked well together."

Justine also went to work for the Nelson Lagoon Council and later the village corporation. Schooled as an artist, with a resume that included belly-dancing, this was yet another improbable move.

"I knew nothing about office skills. I was trained to be an artist or a musician. I was also good at playing the piano at that time. But I learned. Paul and I learned together. And there were a lot of issues that came up in going through all the pains of a corporation or a council and finding your center."

Many of the issues stemming from the land claims settlement took years to resolve. Meanwhile, planned oil development just offshore from Nelson Lagoon further politicized the region and led to creation of the Aleutians East Borough. Justine found herself involved from the beginning. The peninsula was growing. Life was changing.

Electricity was one of the first major shocks to life in Nelson Lagoon. Prior to 1979, villagers operated generators to power their individual homes. For convenience's sake, Paul connected a kill switch from his bedroom so he could turn off the generator when he turned off the lights at night.

Electrifying Nelson Lagoon was not easy. An early attempt

Like most of Nelson Lagoon's 80 to 90 year-round residents, Paul Gundersen was well-equipped to catch Bering Sea salmon. And when he wasn't fishing, or tending to his family, he built a motorized snow sled, complete with cabin and propellor. (Justine Gundersen)

to harness the wind energy so abundant along the peninsula ended in dismal failure. A windmill generator installed in 1978 crumpled like a wilting flower under the strain of the Bering Sea gales, Justine recalls. After that, more conventional diesel generation was installed, not only powering Nelson Lagoon but connecting it with the world.

"When I first moved to Nelson Lagoon, we didn't have a telephone. We had to go over to Port Moller to make a call. But we had a lot of community activity. Someone would get a movie from town, 35 mm. We'd all go over to their house and we'd have popcorn and watch a movie. We'd pay a couple of dollars. It was fun. And then we got telephones in 1979. One phone, really. It was at the community building. And then we got television, and I think that changed the whole structure of the village."

Even something as basic as water changed life in Nelson Lagoon. Prior to the mid-1980s,

when the village was plumbed into freshwater lakes 16 miles away, there was no running water in Nelson Lagoon. Early attempts to drill wells along the sand spit itself produced only brackish water. But having to pack water was part of the glue that held life together in Nelson Lagoon. Villagers, each with their buckets, joined one another to make the routine trips to the "water lakes." Packing was a community affair that ended with something as simple as the turn of the tap.

Other changes, though, brought the community back together. Simple things like a new gym where villagers gathered to play basketball. A planned dock, meanwhile, offers new economic opportunities. Challenges remain, but the years of work paid off for Paul and Justine.

Paul Gundersen died in 1993. He is buried near his home in Nelson Lagoon. For Justine, the work goes on. She was re-elected in fall 1993 to the Aleutians East Borough Assembly. She serves

on the board of the regional economic development corporation. By now, both moves seem more probable for Justine than not. And when she thinks about her life, Justine is certain of how she would like to be known.

"The wife of Paul Gundersen, I think. That's been the highlight of my whole life. Being married to him and living here. I think I kind of, I don't know, I think I was supposed to evolve here in some way. I don't want to sound mystical now, please don't get me wrong, but it was just so comfortable. I never thought for a moment that this was not the place I was supposed to be. Although everybody else thought I was quite crazy for a long, long time. But, yeah, I'd like to be known as Paul's wife.

"People ask me, 'Are you going to leave now?'" Justine laughs. "How can I? I have all my children and grandchildren here. This is where my roots are now. My heart's here." Theo, the son who came with her those many years ago, still lives in Nelson Lagoon where he fishes commercially and is a private pilot.

Justine laughs again. "My life really started here, here in Nelson Lagoon. And it's been an interesting life, certainly."

The Chignik Area

Fishing, families and religions bind the three Chigniks and their westward cousins Perryville and Ivanof Bay. These communities on the Pacific coast shelter commercial salmon fishermen dependent on Chignik sockeye runs.

The villages of Chignik, Chignik Lagoon and Chignik Lake are clustered off the south side of Chignik Bay, about 260 miles southwest of Kodiak.

Chignik sits at the feet of tall mountains at the head of Anchorage Bay, a thumb off Chignik Bay. It is the oldest and largest of the group, with ties to the old Aleut village of Port Moller and to southern Yup'ik villages along Bristol Bay.

Embedded near today's Chignik is a prehistoric village site nearly 1,900 years old. Remains of a late prehistoric Aleut-style house speak to a northerly movement of Aleuts up the Pacific coast. In the 1700s, Russians destroyed a later village, Kaniagmiut, in this locale, according to local lore. An 1881 report spoke of Kaluiak village where Native caribou hunters lived. Collapsed cabins from the early 1900s are visible at abandoned Mud Bay village west of town. Old photos hanging in the Chignik city office show the village's sod homes, or barabaras.

About 177 people, many with Alutiiq ancestry, live in Chignik year-round and keep town going through winter. The population explodes in summer when another 1800 people arrive for salmon season. College students, Mexicans and Filipinos work in Chignik's two processing plants. The hordes of incoming fishermen include affluent Chignik villagers who spend winters in Kodiak, Anchorage or Seattle. Some do this so their children can attend bigger city schools.

The influence of Scandinavian and Russian blood sowed here a century ago shows up in locals as blue eyes and red hair and hints of old-country accents. Some families remain loyal to the region's earliest Christian faith, Russian Orthodoxy. They worship mostly in homes since the church building crumbled. The missionary Chignik Bible Chapel, started here in 1949, offers Sunday services and weekly activities.

Two fish processing plants — Aleutian Dragon Fisheries and Chignik Pride — operate on the waterfront May through October. They process and freeze salmon and halibut, and in a few recent winters handled cod. The plants keep long hours in summer when fishing is most hectic. Seiners clog the bay, rafting seven and eight deep off the cannery docks.

Chignik's fishery is one of the richest and busiest in western Alaska with a fleet of upscale boats, some valued at $750,000. Yet Chignik has no harbor, no public wharf, no breakwater to keep storm swells from sweeping boats into each other, the docks, or the shore. Chignik means "big wind" in Alutiiq.

"We had one big blow last night," said city councilman and boat owner Dick Sharpe in mid-November. "We get some good blows in summertime, too. Then it's really a mess with all the fishing boats. Everyone running around trying to find a place to anchor. There's wrecks of boats all over the bay. A harbor would make a world of difference."

The city of Chignik has long tried to get a breakwater harbor and public dock built. Both

Largest of the three Chignik area communities, Chignik Bay, usually called simply Chignik, straddles a slough at the head of Anchorage Bay. (John Bauman)

may finally materialize within the decade. Barge freight and ferry passengers for the three Chigniks now come across aging cannery docks. Many families transport fishing supplies, household goods and vehicles on the state ferry, which stops here monthly during summer. City officials fear this vital service is jeopardized without a better, larger dock.

Chignik Lagoon village sits on the southeastern shore of Chignik Lagoon, a 7-mile-long body of water stretching between Chignik Bay and Chignik River. This side of the lagoon is known locally as the "flat side," which seems incongruous with the steep mountains lining shore. The village occupies a small shelf of flat terrain, cut in two by the landing strip.

The number of people living in Chignik

Lagoon varies seasonally. The 1990 census tallied 50 year-round residents, but some years the count is higher. The population jumps to several hundred people during fishing season with arrival of the "summerbirds." In good years, this includes many local families returning from winters elsewhere. However in years of poor fish prices like 1993, many of those families stay through winter, unable to afford to leave.

Two miles from the village, across the lagoon on the "cannery side," sits the old Wards Cove Packing Co. (Columbia Ward Fisheries). Years after this facility stopped buying fish, it continued operating the region's best-stocked general store, selling everything from food to boat motors. The

facility abruptly closed in 1993, dismaying local folks. Store manager Wayne Mitchell quickly opened a grocery, deli and general store back in the village. He calls his place "Fresh Stuff," the local nickname for milk and produce.

LEFT: The arrival of the Alaska Marine Highway ferry is one of the highlights of a Chignik summer. The ferry — the Tustumena *made the run in 1993, but a new ferry is scheduled to be launched later in the decade — begins its run at the southcentral Alaska communities of Seward and Homer, continues on to Kodiak, then skips down the Pacific coast of the Alaska Peninsula, cuts over to Sand Point in the Shumagins, then finishes its run at Dutch Harbor in the Aleutians. Vessel traffic was even more important to the Alaska Peninsula a few decades ago, when government ships and private craft hauled all manner of cargo to communities and scattered homesteads along the hundreds of miles of isolated coastline. (Jeff Caven)*

BELOW: The Chignik Community Store, managed by Joann Skonberg, serves Chignik Bay year-round. A branch of the O. Kraft and Son Co. of Kodiak, the Chignik store offers a variety of food and merchandise. Two other stores in Chignik keep summer-only hours: Chignik Pride Fisheries operates a store catering to fishermen, and Rosalie Skonberg has the Chignik Variety Store. (Greg Syverson)

Once a winter trapping camp, Chignik Lake village became a year-round community in the late 1950s when Russian Orthodox families moved here to build a church and school. (Mark Dolan)

Along the beach on the cannery side are numerous fish camp homes occupied in summer by families from Chignik Lake, Perryville and Ivanof Bay. Chignik Lake village, at the mouth of Chignik Lake, is about 10 miles from the fish camps, and linked to the lagoon by the Chignik River.

About 130 people live at the lake village, the most Alutiiq and traditional of the Chigniks. It was just a winter trapping and fishing camp until the late 1950s when Russian Orthodox families settled here permanently to protect their religious identity and get a school for their children.

Prior to this, many of the lake families lived in an old Russian Orthodox village on the sand spit on the lagoon's cannery side. Each spring, families from the old village and relatives from Ilnik, on the Bristol Bay coast, met at fish camp on the lagoon. Their children would attend summer school here. During winter, some of them moved to trapping camps on the lake, sending their children to schools in Port Heiden or Pilot Point.

About the time of statehood, the Russian Orthodox families were urged to move across to Chignik Lagoon village, which had a school. They refused, partly to maintain their religious unity. They moved to the lake and built their own school and church. They were joined at the lake by people from Ilnik, abandoned in the mid-1950s. Dora Artemie Lind Andre, a Chignik Lake villager interviewed in the mid-1980s for a government report, said missionaries flew in to build a school at the lake, but villagers shooed them away.

This newest of the Chigniks keeps most of its people year-round. Johnny and Kathy Lind tend a small store and the post office in the ground floor of their two-story home. The modern school has a gym, greenhouse and teacher's quarters. Steam baths in old-fashioned banyas continue to be popular.

The lake's Russian Orthodox church houses icons from abandoned churches at the old lagoon village and Ilnik. Father Maxim Isaac, the lake's third resident priest, also ministers monthly to Port Heiden, Pilot Point, Perryville and the other two Chigniks.

Subsistence activities in winter — with airplanes, skiffs, all-terrain vehicles and snow machines — brings in caribou, fish and beach foods.

Most Chignik Lake people still spend summers fishing on the lagoon. A few families stay at the lake, working at the post office or school. Frequent boat traffic connects the village and its extended community at the lagoon.

Transporting people, goods and fuel between the three Chigniks currently relies on boats and small planes. The Lake and Peninsula Borough, Alaska's version of a county government, supports a locally generated plan to build a 12-mile gravel road between the bay and lagoon. An extension to the lake could possibly come later, said borough manager Glenn Vernon.

The Chigniks today were shaped by early Russian fur traders, white trappers, Scandinavian and European fishermen who mixed with Alutiiq Natives.

The fur traders came first. Hunting for sea otters, seals and sea lions gave way to trapping land mammals like foxes and minks. By the late 1800s small trapping communities of whites and Natives dotted the Pacific coast.

In 1888, the Fishermen's Packing Co. of Astoria, Ore., prospected for salmon in Chignik Bay, returning with 2,160 barrels of salted fish. The next year, the company built a cannery on the eastern shore of Chignik Lagoon. Two other companies — the Shumagin Packing Co. of Portland and the Chignik Bay Packing Co. of San Francisco — also built canneries there that year. The three firms consolidated and in 1893 joined Alaska Packers Association. The Chignik Bay Co. operated in the lagoon village as late as 1951.

Across the lagoon on its west shore, Harry

The community of Chignik Lagoon sits on a flat shelf of land beneath tall mountains on the eastern side of Chignik Lagoon. (Bill Sherwonit)

W. Crosby built the Chignik Packing Co. cannery in 1932. Kadiak Fisheries Co. bought it in 1947, operating the renamed Chignik Fisheries Co. cannery until 1953. Kadiak then downscaled the facility to supply and service boats only. In 1968, Wards Cove Packing Co. acquired the property as a fish buying station, store and service center. Wards Cove stopped buying fish here in 1990, and closed the facility entirely in spring 1993.

The first canneries went in over at Anchorage Bay in 1896, built by Hume Bros. & Hume, and Pacific Steam Whaling Co. This started the town of Chignik Bay. In 1901, the canneries joined with Pacific Packing and

Navigation Co., and in 1910 became part of Alaska Packers. The company powered and heated its facilities with coal from a Chignik River mine.

Alaska Packers also operated a fish trap and bunkhouse at the mouth of the Aniakchak River, from 1917 through the 1940s. The Carlson family who lived on Kumlik Island tendered the catch to the Chignik cannery.

That cannery burned in July 1976. It was rebuilt and operated during the crab fishing years by new owner Conagra, an agricultural firm out of Omaha, Neb. In 1985, Aleutian Dragon Fisheries began operating the plant. In late 1993, ADF filed for reorganization under Chapter 11.

Chignik's other plant was built by Peter Pan Seafoods in the mid-1970s during the crab fishing boom. A consortium of five village corporations took it over as Chignik Coastal Fisheries Inc. In 1984, it was sold to Bob Resoff, owner of Sea Catch Inc. of Seattle, and renamed Chignik Pride Fisheries.

During the early years, the canneries would bring live goats, sheep, cows, and chickens to butcher and feed summer workers. At the end of the season, the remaining live animals would be given away or sold, starting a local tradition of small-scale livestock farming.

In the early years, most of the canneries' workers were Chinese with some Filipinos and Hawaiians. The fishermen associated with the canneries were mostly Scandinavian, Italian and Greek, with a few Scots and Germans. Some of these foreigners married local Alutiiq women, many of whom had Russian ancestry.

Natives found only a few jobs with the canneries at first, and many continued fur trapping through the 1920s. Some Native families raised foxes on islands near Chignik Bay as late as the 1930s, when fur prices plummeted. These foxes had been put on the islands in 1880 by the Alaska Commercial Co.

Anchored by salmon and canneries, the Chigniks drew people from both sides of the peninsula, as well as fishermen from distant shores. They outlasted other older settlements. Two of these were on Sutwik and Mitrofania islands, where sea otter hunters lived in sod huts and fur trading posts operated. People from these settlements ended up in the Chigniks. The village of Kanatak up the coast north of Chignik boomed temporarily in the early 1920s with oil drilling. A number of Chignik and Chignik Lake residents were born in Kanatak.

Today, the Chignik fishery exerts the same powerful draw on fishermen far and near, particularly from the Alutiiq villages of Perryville and Ivanof Bay, 50 miles westward.

Perryville originated in 1912 as the new home for Katmai villagers displaced by the eruption of Katmai volcano. The government sent the revenue cutter *Manning* to take them to find a new home. They were joined by refugees from Kaguyak (Douglas) village. They sailed into Ivanof Bay, but white trappers there reportedly turned them away with complaints of deep snow and few animals, claims later proved bogus.

They landed in the next bay north, and were put ashore with tents, lumber and a government-sponsored carpenter. They named their new village after the *Manning's* captain, Lt. Cmdr. K.W. Perry. Their journey to safety landed them 250 miles south, yet looming over their new home was another active volcano, Mount Veniaminov.

Perryville residents are almost all Alutiiq. Small houses sit among sand dunes, surrounded by tall grasses and fireweed in summer. Almost every home has a banya for taking steams. Trails through the village are wide enough for the few trucks to pass, but most everyone walks.

The village's 2,500-foot runway allows for regular cargo, mail and passenger flights

from King Salmon. A small grocery store operates from a private home. Two public docks and a boat launch improve the waterfront. Many activities focus on the school. The Kametolook River yields good fishing for food. In summer, almost everyone leaves the village for fish camps on Chignik Lagoon. The people of Perryville are closely linked by culture and blood to Chignik Lake villagers.

In 1965, six families left Perryville in a schism with the Russian Orthodox Church. United by evangelical Protestantism, they started their own community at the head of Ivanof Bay, site of an abandoned cannery.

Perryville originated in 1912 as the new home for people from two villages ruined in the eruption of Katmai volcano. Until his death in 1986, Father Harry Kaiakokonok, Katmai's Russian Orthodox priest, resided here, distinguishing Perryville as the regional seat of Orthodoxy. Its Russian Orthodox church, St. John the Theologian, is on the National Register of Historic Places. (Alaska Volcano Observatory)

Today, the school and village store employ a few of the settlement's 35 residents. Many families migrate to Chignik fish camps in summer. Trapping and subsistence hunting and fishing are important winter activities. ∎

Chignik Summers

By Jane Barnett

Editor's note: *Jane Barnett has spent the past five summers in Chignik, with her fiance, Dan Veerhusen, skipper of the 50-foot purse seiner,* Shady Lady, *and Dan's sons Brett, 8, and Adam, 12. Jane is from Scotland; Dan was born in Seward, Alaska, and raised in Homer. Dan, Brett and Adam helped Jane with this account of summers in Chignik where Dan fishes for Aleutian Dragon Fisheries. The* Shady Lady *carries Chignik on its stern, but Dan and his boat fish throughout Alaska depending on the season. In spring, Dan fishes out of Sitka, then moves to Prince William Sound, to Cook Inlet, to Togiak, then to Chignik for the summer salmon season.*

Flying from King Salmon to Chignik, our first stop is Chignik Lake village, situated at the foot of Chignik Lake and at the head of the Chignik River, a lifeline for area fishermen because its waters carry the salmon upstream to spawn.

Only a few minutes away by plane, the next stop is Chignik Lagoon, host to many of the lake people during summer fishing. The lagoon also has its own year-round community with a school and small store.

Once more down the runway, we head for our final destination, Chignik Bay. The land below is vast. Lush green alders mass the hillsides until they meet the

FAR LEFT: *Jane Barnett; her fiance, Dan Veerhusen; and Dan's sons, Adam, 12, and Brett, 8, show off a king salmon caught while sport fishing in the Chignik River. (Courtesy of Jane Barnett)*

LEFT: *Dan Veerhusen and sons Adam (left) and Brett display some of the fowl they raised during a summer at Chignik. The animals were being transferred to Chignik Lagoon to spend the winter. (Jane Barnett)*

LOWER LEFT: *Chignik Bay's water reservoir is nestled in the mountains behind town. A three-quarter-mile wooden pipe carries water to town by siphoning action. (Greg Syverson)*

alpine meadows. Above the meadows nothing grows; there's just the gray and red craggy tops of the mountains, streaked with leftover snow from the winter past that drains down the many waterfalls that stripe the face.

As the plane lands on the newly repaired runway, trucks and four-wheelers gather, their drivers waiting to greet friends and collect mail. In summer there are generally three or four flights per day into Chignik on PenAir, with a round-trip fare from King Salmon of $320 in 1993. The planes bring in all the mail, which is then distributed to the post office and to both canneries, Chignik Pride Fisheries and Aleutian Dragon Fisheries (ADF). The canneries tend to the fishermen's mail.

I have only flown into Chignik once; the other years I have come from Homer via fishing boat. The trip takes between 32 and 36 hours down Shelikof Strait, with arrival at Chignik between May 27 and June 2.

The salmon fishing season officially runs from June 1 to October 31. Salmon fishing has started as early as June 6; however, this is unusually early and it normally begins between June 16 and 23. The first opening generally only lasts one to two days, depending on fish escapement through the weir. The fishing openings and closings are controlled by the Alaska Department of Fish and Game from counts at their weir below Chignik Lake. Normally the first run lasts about three weeks, sometimes with constant fishing. Then usually the fishing closes for one to two weeks to allow the second run to build. The second run of red salmon is unique to Chignik. Once the escapement is met, fishing may open for five to seven days, then close for two to three days, normally on six- to 24-hours notice. By the time mid-August rolls around, fishermen are generally fishing a steady three to four days. By this time, only about 10 percent to 20 percent of the fish are reds; the rest are pink,

This view from a trail behind town looks out over Anchorage Bay toward Chignik Bay. The docks of Aleutian Dragon Fisheries are at right. (Greg Syverson)

silver and chum (dog) salmon.

There are 102 permits for the Chignik area; about 80 are owned by Natives, the others by fishermen from other areas of Alaska or by Outsiders, mostly from the Seattle area. The district covers a large area; however, the fish only seem to run at certain points. In the past, before Dan started fishing in the area, the lagoon seemed to be the more popular place to fish with shallow draft boats and smaller nets. But as fishing has progressed, larger boats — the state limits salmon seining boats to a maximum of 58 feet — have entered the fishery and many now fish the outside waters. The fishing district stretches from the western point of Kupreanof Peninsula east to Cape Kilokak.

Before the salmon season,

many fishermen go after halibut, which opens for 24 hours about June 8. The halibut opening can be hard to plan because the salmon season can open anytime. After halibut fishing is over, Brett and Adam fly in. I help with the halibut fishing, but when the boys arrive, I head for shore. It seems that when children reach about age 12, if their dads have a boat they are put to work learning the skills involved in fishing. If the weather is good, Dan's boys go out to help on the boat. If the weather turns bad, the fish tenders bring the boys in to the cannery.

Many children have four-wheelers or motorcycles to ride. We ourselves stick to our bicycles, much to the disappointment of the boys who would much rather have something with an engine.

We make at least one trip per day to the airport, about two miles each way, for exercise. On nice days we pack a lunch and spend the day at the lake out by the airport. People don't seem to arrive until afternoon, but when they do come there's lots of activity: all kinds of floating toys, innertubes, even a jet ski or two. People have barbecues and there's lots of laughter.

One of my favorite things to do is round up a few people, some dogs and a gun and hike about one hour to the dam. The trail is steep for the first 15 minutes, then levels out. The trail follows a pipeline that carries water from the dam to the ADF cannery. It's about two and one-half miles to the dam the short way, following the pipeline. The long way, about three miles, requires fording a river. We make lots of noise to let the bears know we are around. We have a picnic, usually just sandwiches because of the bears. Then we target practice, normally aiming for a distant rock. Our other days are spent fishing off ADF's dock or at the hole in the wall, an opening in the rock at cliffs about one-half mile from town. We catch Dolly Varden there and even the odd halibut. We like to pick wildflowers, and salmonberries when they are ripe.

Fourth of July, Camp Fire, the water safety course, Bible camp and Wacky Wednesday provide other events for a Chignik summer.

At Fourth of July, some years there are events; other years nothing much goes on. In 1993,

The most inland of three communities clustered in the Chignik area, the buildings of Chignik Lake are scattered along the shore of the lake, connected to Chignik Bay by the Chignik River. Inland from Chignik Lake lies Black Lake. Footprints from two types of dinosaurs from the Jurassic period (144 to 218 million years ago) have been found near this lake. These finds are the oldest known dinosaur finds in Alaska, but little is yet known about them. (Jane Barnett)

the community organized a small parade for the children, some races, and fun and games inside the community hall. Then ADF offered a free lunch. That night there was a talent show for anyone who wanted to participate, followed by a dance. Tony Gregorio's band, whose leader is a fisherman from Chignik Lagoon, played at this dance and all the other dances held during the summer. Fireworks normally start about two weeks before the Fourth and continue for about two weeks after. When residents hear the name Snake Eyes, they know the fireworks have arrived. Snake Eyes, whose real name is Sam Egli, takes his name from his call sign. He flies in from Naknek, spreads his fireworks on the parking area at the airport, and villagers come by to buy them.

The non-denominational Christian church offers activities for the children. Missionaries come for the summer, normally a different family each season. They organize Wacky Wednesday with games, stories and crafts for all

ages from 2 p.m. to 4 p.m. For a week each summer the missionaries open a Bible camp, an expanded version of Wacky Wednesday, when they may put on a play, and offer prizes at the end of the week for learning Bible verses.

Although they did not come to Chignik Bay in summer 1993, representatives from Camp Fire, usually two college students, visit most summers, organizing games and crafts for the children.

It seems the Camp Fire activities alternate with the water safety course at which films on water safety are shown. After basic instruction, students go to the airport lake to learn to swim and to try out wet suits and survival suits…weather permitting. Occasionally it's just too windy and too cold for the

children to be going in and out of the water.

Sometimes the Chignik Tribal Council hires employees to teach crafts to the children. With all these things to do, we keep quite busy. And it doesn't get dark until 1 a.m. in the summer so we have many late nights.

At other times, if fishing closes for a week or so between runs, we leave our summer home, a trailer, load our kayaks and bikes onto the *Shady Lady* and run to Sand Point, for a few days. The trip takes eight hours to the end of Kupreanof Peninsula and another four hours to Sand Point.

Another traditional outing is to go up the river to Chignik Lake and fish for kings. We leave the *Shady Lady* at the head of the lagoon — we can only go in around high tide — and

take the skiff upriver.

We have two main stores at Chignik Bay. Both keep a good stock, from rain gear to Haagen Dazs ice cream. Coastal Transportation's boat out of Seattle brings in fresh fruit and vegetables and general groceries once a week. Many local people and fishermen order their main supplies from companies in Seattle such as Span Alaska and Arts, who ship on Coastal Transportation. Rosalie Skonberg runs a variety store out of her home that sells jewelry, T-shirts, music tapes etc., and Florence Skonberg operates a bakery that sells homemade donuts and bread, quite a treat for a rural area. I guess you could say we have three cafes. The first is the local cafe, run by members of the Carlson family, which serves good food and is normally open for all three meals daily. The other two places to eat are the two canneries. For $7.50 the cannery will provide a meal. The canneries close during the winter, except for cod, and few local people work at the canneries.

The ferry comes into Chignik Bay once a month from spring to fall. It arrives in Chignik normally around 3 a.m. to 4 a.m., and continues on to Dutch Harbor. On its return, it stops in Chignik in the afternoon. The ferry's arrival is a highlight of Chignik life. Everyone comes down to see what's happening. The tourists flood town, coming back with T-shirts, souvenirs and smoked salmon. Then the tourists reboard and are gone, and Chignik goes back to its quiet ways.

Port Heiden

The old village of Meshik and its newer neighbor Port Heiden coalesce into a single community on the Alaska Peninsula's north shore. Visible on clear days, Aniakchak caldera rises 10 miles to the east. Adventurous souls sometimes land at Port Heiden's big airfield and hike up the river drainages to the caldera's rim.

During the summer, however, these visitors would find residents focused on the sea. Most of the 125 people who live here are commercial salmon fishermen.

Like elsewhere on the peninsula, most everyone in Meshik is related by blood or marriage, with kinfolk throughout the region. Scandinavian heritage runs several generations deep, intertwined with Alutiiq or Aleut.

Fishing for cod, then salmon, in Bristol Bay brought Scandinavian fishermen to Meshik around the turn of the century. The village sat on a sandy beach of a bay off the Bering Sea.

To early Natives traveling along the peninsula's northern coast, the bay probably appeared like an obvious place to set up camp. It's the only natural, albeit shallow, harbor between Port Moller and Ugashik Bay, a span of about 140 miles. A small island close to shore within the bay acted as a breakwater, shielding the beach from tide waters and storm waves. Seals hauled out on the island. Just inland from the beach lay freshwater Goldfish Lake.

The 1880 census found 40 people in Meshik, a decade later the population was nearly double. The growth apparently continued; Meshik was "very large" during the early 1900s, according to local people interviewed for a 1982 government report. Meshik had a post office from 1912 to 1915.

The early 1900s brought change throughout the peninsula. Fishing companies from large consortiums to small independents descended to cash in on Bristol Bay's salmon runs. Fish traps, salteries and canneries sprung up where salmon ran thickest. Many newcomers came with the canneries.

Waves of infectious diseases decimated many peninsula communities around this time. Meshik was hit hard by influenza in 1918, and many died. Survivors from Unangashak, 20 miles away at the east end of the lagoon behind Seal Islands, adopted Meshik as their new home. Yet, the village

In many Alaska Peninsula villages, Russian Orthodox churches with their classic onion domes stand as a distinctive legacy to the earliest foreign influence. As part of Russian colonization led by fur traders to Alaska's southwestern coastal regions, Orthodox priests reached the peninsula in the early 1800s. The religion they left behind still plays an important part in the lives of many peninsula residents, including those at Port Heiden who attend this Russian Orthodox church and honor their dead with traditional Orthodox burial. (Bill Sherwonit)

Port Heiden mayor Hank Matson stands beside the community's fire engine, which was obtained in 1985 through a legislative grant and then delivered by barge. (Mark Dolan)

only echoed its former strength with 30 people in 1920.

Port Heiden Packing Co. operated a saltery in Meshik until the 1930s, but the shallow bay apparently discouraged construction of a cannery. The saltery hired some local people, paying them in tokens rather than cash.

Canneries on the Ugashik River drew some Meshik men to work. But generally, locals found few jobs with the canneries. Some Natives trapped small game for fur pelts to trade or sell. Others trapped foxes that had been transplanted onto offshore islands to raise for pelts.

World War II brought another batch of newcomers to Meshik when the military built Fort Morrow up the coast about five miles. Some 5,000 men were stationed here during the 1940s. The base was demobilized after the war, and the site served the White Alice communications network until the mid-1970s.

The military's legacy to the community was 60 miles of road and the Port Heiden Airfield, with a 6,200-foot gravel landing strip and a crosswind runway. Originally designed to support strategic bases in the Aleutian Islands, the airfield today gives Port Heiden uncommonly good access for Bush Alaska. It serves as a small regional hub for passengers, mail and freight with regularly scheduled flights. A road connects the airfield to the old village of Meshik.

Few families live today in Meshik, which is being severely eroded by tides and storms; the small breakwater island has mostly washed away although harbor seals still haul out here. Most everyone has moved up the road north, to homes in two government housing projects. Old Hud is a couple of miles from the old village. Most of the town's commercial and public buildings sit along the Old Hud turnoff. New Hud is a few miles farther up the main road, in a development east of the airfield.

The community is so spread out that it takes school bus driver Roxanne Shade about four and one-half hours to run her route each day for 35 students. The Meshik School, built about 1980, sits about a mile north of the old village, where relics of the original school building can be found. A new addition to the current school, including classrooms to replace old trailers, may be ready by fall 1995.

The school serves as a community hall, hosting roller skating, movies, cake walks, family dinners and public meetings.

The main part of town near Old Hud consists of Hank's Hardware and a grocery/ general store called Jack's New Meshik Mall, the city office, post office, fire barn, Russian Orthodox church and a non-denominational chapel. A third store, Anna Mae's Gift Shop, is still located in the old village. All three of the retail businesses are owned by the same person.

A uniquely important entity is Christensen and Sons Fish Co. Annie and John Christensen opened the business in 1973 to buy locally caught silver salmon, providing a market for fish ignored by other buyers more interested in Bristol Bay sockeye. They iced the fish for air shipment to wholesalers in Anchorage. Now the Christensen's "fish house" buys kings and silvers to ice and fly out in 2,000-pound totes. The Christensens and their five children also fish commercially.

Fishing starts in late May with king salmon. Fishermen use drift gillnets from boats in the bay, and some of them setnet from shore.

In July, most Port Heiden fishermen migrate north to Pilot Point, to fish for Bristol Bay sockeye at Ugashik. At the same time, south peninsula fishermen arrive in Port Heiden to do drift netting. Most of the south peninsula fishermen live on their boats, coming into town occasionally to shop, post mail and pick up supplies at the airfield. A taxi ferries the fishermen from the beach to town.

In August, Port Heiden fishermen come home. They fish through September for local silver salmon.

The Meshik River, a spawning ground for kings and silvers, empties into the bay, forming a silty delta at its mouth. The river starts on the south slopes of the caldera. Fed by streams and shallow Meshik Lake, it courses south, then west, in braided fashion through a broad, marshy valley to the coast.

Moose and caribou migrate through the valley. Some wolves, beaver, river otter, mink, weasels and fox, along with a few lynx and wolverine, range through the region. The river's salmon draw brown bears in summer from their spring feeding areas along the coast north of town. The concentration of game and the convenience of Port Heiden's airfield bring a handful of hunting guides and their clients to the area each fall.

Pilot Point/Ugashik

The Ugashik River meanders across flat, marshy tundra and empties into Ugashik Bay, a major cleft in the eastern shore of Bristol Bay.

The river flows from Upper and Lower Ugashik lakes, scooped out by glaciers during the last ice age. Fingers of land pinch the lakes apart, except for a slender waterway, the Ugashik Narrows. People lived along these narrows almost continuously going back 9,000 years, the oldest site of human habitation known on the Alaska Peninsula.

Today, most everyone on the Ugashik drainage lives near the mouth of the river at Pilot Point, on the eastern shore of Ugashik Bay. The older Native village of Ugashik, about 15 miles upriver, is all but deserted except in summer when commercial salmon fishermen descend. Both communities depend on airplanes and boats for passenger, freight and fuel service because they have no highways out.

The Ugashik River is one of Bristol Bay's great sockeye salmon producers. Its salmon drew some of western Alaska's earliest processors. The Alaska Packers' Ugashik Fishing Station cannery opened in 1894. At the time, the small cannery community was known as Pilot Station because of a Native resident who piloted boats through the main channel of the river's entrance. Its name changed to Pilot Point in 1933.

Canneries also were built near Ugashik around the turn of the century. Ugashik was the big settlement on the river until the influenza epidemic of 1918-19 so decimated the village that most of the survivors moved to the Pilot Point fish camp.

Chinese cannery workers lived in one section of the camp, known as China Town. Italian fishermen beached their boats in a creek still known as Dago Creek. In 1923, a group of Inupiat Eskimos arrived, and they

lived separate in Eskimo Town. They herded reindeer in their early years at Pilot Point, but then let the reindeer loose to mix with the peninsula's caribou, according to local memories.

Sometime early this century a German named Gust Griechen arrived in Pilot Point as a winter watchman for the Alaska Packer's cannery. He had fled Germany by stowing away on a sailing ship. He came ashore in New York, joined the merchant marine, and eventually hooked up with Alaska Packers in San Francisco. He served as winter watchman at the Alaska Packer's cannery in Pilot Point for 50 years, a job subsequently taken by two of his sons until Alaska Packers sold out in the late 1970s.

Today, his grandson Sonny Griechen serves as Pilot Point's first mayor. The town incorporated in 1992, so it could raise tax money for improvements. A 3 percent tax on fish was overwhelmingly approved by the 40 townspeople who voted. In the two years since its

About 97 people, half of whom are school-age children, live year-round in the Alutiiq village of Pilot Point, seen here from the airport road. The population climbs to nearly 2,000 people in summer, with crews from fishing boats and floating fish processors. No processors operate on shore in Pilot Point. (Mark Dolan)

passage, the fish tax has generated $900,000, revenue that has allowed the city to run electricity and water to the waterfront, and to provide ice for fishermen to chill their catch and keep it in better condition to get higher prices from the buyers. The city also started garbage pick-up, a retail fuel outlet, and is upgrading 14 miles of trails around town. A fourth of the tax is stashed in an investment fund to be used in voter-approved capitol improvements. Another 3 percent goes into an educational endowment for scholarships and vocational programs, like a popular computer class offered in winter.

Pilot Point has few businesses. The Griechen family has operated the Pilot Point Trading Post for about 20 years, but planned to close it in 1994, unable to compete with lower cost groceries that most residents get by mail from Anchorage.

Harold Griechen, Sonny's brother, runs a bed and breakfast called Caribou Lookout Lodge. It's particularly popular with sport hunting guides who work out of Pilot Point in fall and winter.

The town sits atop a bluff overlooking the bay. The old cannery was on the beach below, but only ruins remain. An old Russian

Orthodox church, on the National Register of Historic Places, rises in the center of town.

The town's first school, built in 1939, is to be soon replaced with one that will include a gym, allowing Pilot Point students to form school basketball and volleyball teams for the first time.

Orin Seybert, founder of Peninsula Airways (PenAir), came to Pilot Point as a youngster with his parents, who taught at the school four years. Seybert earned money fishing in Bristol Bay during summers to pay for flying lessons and his first plane, which he flew to Pilot Point after high school graduation in Seattle. He landed on the beach, like he'd seen other pilots there do. "For the first years, my most important book was the tide book," he recalled recently.

He started flying sick people from Chignik, Pilot Point and King Salmon up to the Native hospital at Dillingham and soon got his commercial license. He married Jennie Andre,

LEFT: Andrew and Sophie Abyo reside in Pilot Point, a coastal village originally known as Pilot Station. Born at the nearby settlement of Ugashik in 1942, Andrew is the village council president and is also employed by the Bristol Bay Native Association as a tribal child-service worker. Sophie, born in 1941 at Chignik Lake, worked as Pilot Point's community health aide from 1971 to 1981. (Mark Dolan)

LOWER LEFT: Contestants in the sleeping bag race, one of several activities during Pilot Point's winter festival, jumped out of their sleeping bags, built fires for tea, packed up their camps, and raced their four-wheelers and snow machines around a course. "Some couldn't get their fires built or keep them going. It was hilarious," said Sue Evanoff, village health aide and a member of the Sisterhood of St. Nicholas Church, which sponsored the festival. A smelting derby at nearby Ugashik village was another popular event during 1993's first annual festival. (Bill Sherwonit)

an Aleut from Chignik, and they settled in Pilot Point. The business grew, catering in part to fishermen and processors. Today his company flies passengers and freight throughout western Alaska with headquarters in Anchorage. Seybert maintains a home and voting residency in Pilot Point.

Sonny's dad, Gust Griechen Jr., or Ace as he's known, flew 30 years for Seybert until he retired recently.

Seybert's daughter, Cecelia, is president of the Pilot Point Native Corp., the village corporation that owns much of the local land. She and her husband, Emil Christensen from Port Heiden, and their children, fish for herring and salmon in Bristol Bay. Cecelia often flies her plane to spot fish for their boat.

Up river at Ugashik, winters are even more quiet. David Matsuno, the 34-year-old son of a large fishing family, is about the only year-round inhabitant. He does some hunting and trapping, accompanied by his two dogs. Sometimes after the river freezes, he walks down to Pilot Point for an evening of pinochle.

In summer, some 60 people — including David's mother and adult brothers and sisters — return to Ugashik for setnet fishing. Many of them grew up there. A few of them return in winter occasionally to check their cabins.

In summer 1993, Ugashik resident Roland Briggs took over his parents' custom salmon canning business. Beginning in 1961, the Briggs-Way Co. has produced hand-packed red salmon in glass jars for a mail order market. Roland renamed the company Ugashik Wild Salmon and stepped up production in his first summer of ownership, expanding into the gourmet food market. He buys the fish from Ugashik setnetters, sending some out fresh by air to wholesalers and canning the rest in the company's signature glass jars. In this remote region of peninsula wetlands, Briggs is yet another entrepreneur making his way among the salmon. ■

Egegik

The small village of Egegik becomes a madhouse in summer when sockeye salmon return to Bristol Bay. For a few frantic weeks, the community swarms with commercial fishermen, fish buyers and processing workers cashing in on one of the West Coast's hottest fisheries.

Record catches during the early 1990s — including 21.8 million sockeye in 1993, a quarter of the entire West Coast harvest — cemented Egegik's status. Some 900 boats, several dozen fish tenders, and a couple thousand people showed up to fish out of Egegik. An even bigger harvest is predicted for 1994.

"In summer, the village gets full," declares Margo Schoonmaker, a Native setnetter who lives in Anchorage during winter. She and her sister Hazel Nelson setnet each summer out of Egegik. They take food and fuel to their cabin, along with every piece of rain gear imaginable. "It's very hard work but to me, it's wonderful," Schoonmaker says. "It gets in your blood and you just can't let go of it."

Egegik's seemingly remote location and usual quiet countenance belie its summertime frenzy. For most of the year, it is a laid-back village of about 120 people.

Only one store operates through winter, so residents mostly shop by mail. Airplanes and boats transport people and goods since no roads lead out of town. Egegik's Russian Orthodox church is on the National Register of Historic Places, but has no resident priest. Most of the community's attention focuses on school with occasional gatherings at the community hall.

People hunt, fish and pick berries, partly out of tradition and also to cut grocery costs. There are few cash jobs in the community. Here, as in many peninsula fishing towns, annual incomes for many people fall beneath poverty level. Hunting and fishing for food take on added importance.

The village sits at the mouth of the Egegik River on the south shore of Egegik Bay. The river flows from Becharof Lake, cascading over rocks into a small lagoon then meandering through marshy tundra to the coast. It is joined near its mouth by the King Salmon River out of the mountains to the east. Caribou and moose frequent the region, along with beaver, fox, ptarmigan, wolverine and brown bear.

Winter freeze-up opens the countryside to all-terrain vehicles and snow machines. People sometimes still take a 50-mile winter coastal trail between Egegik and South Naknek, a main mail route earlier this century. From Kanatak Bay on the Pacific side, sled dog teams carried mail across frozen Becharof Lake to Ugashik and Egegik, then up to South Naknek along the coastal trail, and on to Dillingham.

For most of the year, Egegik's only store is the Egegik Trading Co., which carries groceries, lumber, hardware and building supplies. Owner Dick Deigh, a driftnet fisherman and president of both the Egegik Village Council and Egegik Improvement Corp., keeps abbreviated winter hours. He

The village of Egegik sits at the mouth of Egegik River on the south shore of Egegik Bay. It has existed here since the late 1800s, although many older sites along the river mark earlier Alutiiq villages. The current site was a Native fish camp as early as 1876. In 1895, the Alaska Packers Association started a salmon saltery here. During the 1918 influenza epidemic, Natives from other villages moved to Egegik to escape the disease. Egegik also drew Scandinavian fishermen who married Alutiiq women, some with Russian ancestry. (Hazel Nelson)

This closeup aerial of Egegik shows Nelbro Packing Co. buildings and dock in spring 1993. The company, one of several fish processing facilities in Egegik, since has built a new, two-story bunkhouse. Behind the Nelbro complex is a local natural feature called Grandma's Lake that used to have land-locked salmon. (Hazel Nelson)

opens at 1 p.m. and closes when the last person leaves. "We have these people trained," he jokes. "They show up when we open, buy their stuff and get out." The store stays open all day in summer to accommodate Egegik's near non-stop activity. A pizza parlor, a few boat repair shops and marine supply stores are also open then.

The first fishermen arrive in April, for the herring season at Togiak. Things stay busy through September, when guides bring sport hunters through town. Hunters must first obtain a recreational license from the village's Becharof Corp. before entering corporation lands.

Salmon season June through August turns Egegik into a small city of 1,000 to 3,000 people. Its landing strip churns with small planes bringing people, baggage, freight and mail.

A new state runway is going in two miles east of town in 1994, and the village council is planning a public dock. Egegik residents intend to incorporate as a city to collect a sales tax on fish. The revenue could help Egegik develop into a regional service hub, says Hazel Nelson, president of Becharof Corp.

Four companies run fish camps during summer at former Egegik cannery sites. Woodbine Alaska Fish and Nelbro Packing have small stores, washaterias and cafes. Wards Cove Packing offers similar services across the river, as does Peter Pan Seafoods at Coffee Point, on the north shore of Egegik Bay. Woodbine still freezes and cans fish in Egegik, but the others send fish to processing plants elsewhere.

Coffee Point bustles during sockeye season. Setnetters line the beach, and small planes spotting fish for the driftnet fleet buzz overhead. Skiffs ferry fishermen ashore to do business with fish buyers and Peter Pan. The Becharof Corp. continues developing its property on the point, and leased land to Peter Pan for a new runway for fish and freight. The airstrip helps alleviate dangerous congestion on the beach caused by planes landing among setnet lines and people.

Red Clark of Naknek has fished off Coffee Point for several decades. He recalls when few setnetters worked here and the beach was practically empty. During the early years of the Bristol Bay fishery, the canneries controlled the fleet, cutting nets and stealing fish to intimidate independent fishermen such as himself, Clark says. Sometimes disputes were settled at gunpoint.

Egegik's fishery today is nearly as lawless, he says, particularly on the north line where boats jostle for position. "They pull guns on one another right and left," he says. "It's a hell of a place in summer."

Back in the village, Deigh agrees. He driftnets in the river, content to leave the north marker craziness to others. "You have to see it to believe it," he says, "and then when you see it, you go away mumbling.

They cut nets, they ram each other. There's lots of aluminum boats with battle scars. I've been out there a couple of times and that's enough. It's where you meet your friends and create enemies."

The fishing crowds spelled opportunity for Red Clark's daughter and granddaughter in summer 1993. Mary Clark Underwood and daughter Lynn, who have setnet permits for Egegik, opened an espresso stand near Coffee Point. The fishermen from Seattle, where espresso flows like water, couldn't believe their binoculars as they surveyed the beach from offshore. In two weeks of operation, the stand went through 150 pounds of coffee. "Alaska truly is the last frontier," Underwood asserts. "Anybody with a little imagination and initiative can make it."

Just as Egegik's salmon attract hordes of human fishermen, they also draw droves of bears. Egegik bear stories abound. Nelson, whose family homesteaded both sides of the river, grew up in the company of big browns. A bear once stole a plate of pork chops off the front porch, minutes after it had been set out for the family's lunch. The bear peeked in the kitchen window at Hazel's mom, who grabbed a broom to shoo it off. As she ran out the front door, the bear was disappearing with a mouthful of pork.

Even today, the bears roam age-old trails along the river, despite the crowds of people. "The bears pick the fish from our nets," Nelson says. "We have to be especially careful going out at night because of them."

Almost every summer there are close encounters between bears and outsiders, particularly the city folk who like to jog. They often follow the road out of town, not realizing it goes to the dump where bears hang out. Last summer, a dump bear chased a jogger, who was rescued by a local man passing in a truck. By that point, said Nelson, the jogger was running for his life. ∎

The Nakneks and King Salmon

Summer brings extra people to almost every Alaska Peninsula fishing town, but none see crowds like the communities of Naknek, South Naknek and King Salmon.

About 1,450 people live year-round in the three towns, but summertime populations skyrocket to between 15,000 and 20,000, according to estimates by local government officials. They say getting an exact count of seasonal visitors is practically impossible. Most of the summer people come for commercial sockeye salmon fishing. They work on fishing boats, floating and onshore processors, and in the many support services in Naknek.

The seasonal influx also includes tourists to nearby Katmai National Park and Preserve and sport hunters and fishermen coming to area lodges.

Naknek and South Naknek hug opposite shores at the mouth of the Naknek River, a major Bristol Bay sockeye salmon producer at the top of the Alaska Peninsula. King Salmon sits about 15 miles inland on the river's north bank.

Together, the three communities form Bristol Bay Borough, Alaska's equivalent to a county government. This is the state's oldest borough, formed in 1962 by residents wanting control of their schools. It is also the state's smallest borough with 531 square miles of land and 669 square miles of water. It extends from the western boundary of Katmai park to the northwestern shore of Kvichak Bay. The borough offices are located in Naknek.

Commercial fishing takes center stage in Naknek and South Naknek, where 10 fish processing plants operate, some in turn-of-the-century cannery complexes. The first cannery on the Naknek River started up in 1890, and others quickly followed.

Today Naknek is a regional fishing hub

for eastern Bristol Bay, a role it has assumed increasingly during the past decade. In addition to the canneries, it hosts a growing complex of marine industrial support businesses. Welding, painting, net hanging and motor repair shops and several boat storage businesses occupy land around Leader Creek, a protected harbor area on the east edge of Naknek.

Boat traffic congests Naknek River during summer. Dozens of tenders and floating processors work in the bay alongside hundreds of fishing boats. Cannery docks along the river stay busy, and few mooring sites are available. The borough recently built a new dock in South Naknek, and the Naknek village corporation Paug-Vik Inc. Ltd. plans to build a dock in Naknek. Docks at the borough's Port of Bristol Bay in Naknek stay busy with freight barges and fishing boats.

The borough collects a 3 percent raw fish tax, which has provided considerable income for improvements. Those include an indoor swimming pool in Naknek for public use,

Naknek (foreground) and South Naknek hug opposite shores at the mouth of the Naknek River, one of Bristol Bay's top sockeye salmon producers. The river stays open with floating ice at its mouth in winter because of tidal action, although it freezes solid beginning about eight miles upstream. Local residents are split over the idea of building a bridge to connect the communities. (Mark Dolan)

sewers in each community, and a new gym at the borough high school.

John "Smiley" Knutsen, an Aleut drift gillnetter and president of the village corporation, grew up in Naknek. He and his wife, Maureen, live here year-round. Among other things, they are involved in the Bristol Bay Historical Society that runs a museum in the old Fisherman's Hall in Naknek. He has learned much about the region's history from his "grandpappy," Paul Chukan, 93, and grandmother, Anna, 88. Chukan trapped and hunted until he began commercial fishing about World War II. Before the war and its labor shortages, Alaska Natives were pretty much excluded from the industry by the canneries that imported most of their fishermen and workers.

Knutsen began fishing as a child with Chukan. He has seen lots of changes. In the last few years, the trend has been falling fish prices and escalating permit and boat costs. Fish prices fell to 60 cents a pound in 1993 from a high of about $2.40 a pound in the 1980s. With permits priced at $172,000 and new aluminum boats costing $350,000, fishermen — particularly the highly leveraged young ones — have to catch a lot of fish to pay their bills.

"The philosophy of fishing has changed,"

Katmai Air flies visitors to Katmai National Park, east and south of King Salmon, from their station on the Naknek River. During the height of the sport fishing and tourism season each summer, floatplanes lines the river's banks. (Penny Rennick)

Knutsen says. "It used to be a gentlemen's fishery. You'd lay out a net and wait until someone drifted on the line to take your turn. Now it's a combat fishery...there's just no describing what happens. Boats ramming each other. Last year one guy broke his back, another ripped off his thumb. Several broke arms and legs."

State fisheries authorities issue hundreds of tickets each season and fines can reach $15,000. "It's mostly the younger generation," says Knutsen. "Fishermen who've been here 20 and 30 years, we know where the fish are and don't need to be down on the line."

A new fisheries program is providing some local salmon fishermen with alternative jobs during winter. Donald Nielsen Jr., a 25-year-old South Naknek commercial salmon fishermen, has sailed three times on a factory trawler in the Bering Sea. He's participating in a joint venture between Oceantrawl Inc. and the Bristol Bay Economic Development Corp., one of six regional groups representing

Alaska villages in community development quotas for Bering Sea pollock, part of a federal allocation program. Nielsen spends 45 days a stretch on board the 341-foot ship. So far, he has worked in the ship's fish processing factory, alongside dozens of other people. His goal is to become part of the fishing crew on deck. "As a commercial fisherman myself, I would not be happy to be stuck down in the factory the whole time," he said. "Most all the fishermen want to be up on the deck where they're comfortable. But right now it's providing me a little winter income that otherwise wouldn't be there."

The story of King Salmon deviates from fishing. King Salmon grew out of World War II, when the military built a big airfield here as a refueling and rest station in support of strategic bases farther west.

The state now owns the airfield, a transportation hub for the peninsula and Bristol Bay. Airport activity surges in summer with people, fish and freight shipments.

The Federal Aviation Administration, U.S. Fish and Wildlife Service and National Park Service maintain regional offices here, making King Salmon largely a government town. With the headquarters for Katmai National Park and Preserve, King Salmon bills itself as the "gateway to Katmai." Visitors headed to Katmai's Brooks River for bear viewing and fishing catch floatplane charters in King Salmon. Primitive roads from King Salmon also lead to cabins on the park's western border. The town also has an auto parts franchise, a travel agency, a bank, two groceries, a hotel and several restaurants.

For many years, King Salmon was synonymous with the U.S. Air Force, which operated the base. In recent years, the King Salmon facility was a remote duty station for fighter jets out of Elmendorf Air Force Base in Anchorage. In 1994, the Air Force began closing the base and moving out about 260

military personnel. The Alaska Air National Guard plans to maintain the base with about 40 civilian and uniformed personnel to keep it ready for training exercises and emergency use, pending Congressional approval.

Local residents lamented possibly losing access to certain recreation facilities with the Air Force's departure, since the base has the area's only bowling alley, theater and racquetball courts. King Salmon businesses that employed off-duty GIs anticipated difficulty finding replacement workers for their low-paying part-time jobs. Some residents welcomed the exodus of military people who competed for local moose, caribou and fish.

A narrow, 15-mile state road connects Naknek and King Salmon. The state transportation department plans in 1994 to rebuild and widen this thoroughfare, which is so rutted that locals routinely drive on the wrong side to lessen the jolts. They swerve back into the right lanes as needed to accommodate oncoming traffic.

The Bristol Bay Borough School District buses students daily from King Salmon to Naknek, where the schools are located.

South Naknek has no road connection to the other two towns, however. People have discussed, off and on for years, building a river bridge to Naknek. The idea splits the community; it is not popular with some South Naknek residents who like their relative isolation.

In late winter, the river usually freezes solid starting about eight miles above South Naknek, at abandoned Savonoski village. This village was settled in 1912 by people fleeing old Savonoski, east of Naknek Lake, during the eruption of Katmai volcano. Most of the Savonoski villagers later moved to South Naknek, leaving behind a cemetery, old Russian Orthodox church and some other buildings.

RIGHT: The tranquility of this scene of fish processing plants lining the Naknek River at Naknek belies the frenzy that erupts when the salmon are running. Naknek, seat of the Bristol Bay Borough, and South Naknek depend on the fish to sustain their economy. King Salmon, farther upriver, has a more diversified economy, although here too the fish resource indirectly supports the economy. King Salmon looks to transportation, tourism and sport fishing to generate revenue, especially since their military base will be downsized and taken over by the Alaska Air National Guard in 1994. (Penny Rennick)

LOWER RIGHT: A common merganser and chicks sun themselves at Naknek Lake. (David E. Trask)

When the river freezes, Savonoski becomes a departure point for people driving across the ice to the Naknek-King Salmon highway. One reason to cross the river is Winterfest, a festival in King Salmon in early February that offers sled dog races, basketball tournaments, ice golfing, trips to Hawaii and other attractions designed to break up winter. Summer's Fishtival celebrates the end of sockeye season with similar, albeit warm-weather, activities. Boats provide summer river crossings.

Neither ice roads nor boats work for transporting South Naknek students to school in Naknek, however. A 26-foot tidal surge prevents the river from freezing at the villages, and floating ice during the school year makes boat crossings too hazardous. The district contracts an air taxi service to fly the students instead.

"They've been doing this for 30 years, and as far as I know, it's unique, using an airplane for a school bus on a regular basis," says Richard Leath, Bristol Bay Borough school superintendent.

About 20 South Naknek students, sixth to 12th grades, are flown to school in Naknek each day in six-seater airplanes. If they can't get across in the mornings by 11 a.m. because of fog or other bad weather, they go to the South Naknek elementary school where they receive assignments by fax. If they make it across in the morning but weather prevents afternoon flights, the students stay overnight in Naknek at "bad weather homes."

South Naknek students who play basketball stay in Naknek all week and fly home on weekends. The school district pays for food, lodging and airfare of the South Naknek students. It's all part of the district's considerable transportation budget. ■

Fishing Alaska Peninsula Waters

The Alaska Peninsula protrudes between the rich fishing grounds of the North Pacific Ocean and the Bering Sea. With salt water on three sides, 2,800 miles of coastline, and numerous freshwater lakes and rivers, it should be no surprise that life on the Alaska Peninsula revolves around what swims past its shores.

People here spend a lot of time fishing, getting ready to fish, or thinking about fishing. They fish for profit, for food, for sport. They catch mostly salmon, but also Pacific cod, halibut, pollock, crab and a smorgasbord of other finned and shelled fish. They do this in consistently wicked weather. Storms off the oceans routinely slam this mountain-spined arm, and gale-force winds whip waves into boat-size tumblers. Fog and rain are near-constant companions.

Some 340 species of marine life inhabit the peninsula's near and offshore waters. Of the 30 or so commercially valuable species, salmon are the single most important. The past and future of almost every town on the peninsula is tied to the reds, pinks, silvers,

kings and chums that find their way back to western Alaska each year. Salmon fishing and processing is the peninsula's biggest business.

The region's great salmon runs lured the first fish buyers more than a century ago. Their canneries spawned jobs and towns and spurred the salmon industry that prevails today. The peninsula's salmon — its Bristol Bay and Chignik sockeye — are prized among the world's best for taste and color, like vintage wines of the saltwater cellar. Naknek, South Naknek and King Salmon, fishing towns at the top of the peninsula's north side, proclaim themselves "Sockeye Salmon Capital."

Meanwhile, other fish come and go in their commercial importance, and some come again. Sand Point traces its beginnings to commercial codfishing. Today, Pacific cod is again important to Sand Point, as well as King Cove, where large seafood processors operate. These processors depend on cod, pollock, halibut, sablefish and crab to stay busy outside the salmon season.

In some parts of the Alaska Peninsula,

sport fishing brings steady summer business. Posh remote lodges attract well-heeled clients, many from outside the state, who fish for rainbow, grayling, arctic char, lake trout and salmon. These sport fishermen spend upwards of $3,800 a week for food and accommodations, air charters and fishing guides. Some of this money circulates locally, and the lodges employ a limited number of local people seasonally.

Whether boat owners or crew members, cannery workers or storekeepers, professionals, laborers, government bureaucrats or elected officials, residents of the Alaska Peninsula live constantly with the ups and downs of their

These fishing boats are waiting to take their turn at the bar at Chignik Lagoon. They wait here until the tide is right, usually about two hours into the ebb tide, until they spot the fish jumping. Then, one at a time, they release their net, which is called making a set. The waiting boats sometimes harass the boat whose turn it is to make the set. (Jeff Caven)

dominant industry. Salmon crashes of 1973 and 1974 brought federal disaster aid to the region. Record runs and prices brought prosperity in the 1980s. In summer 1989, oil from the *Exxon Valdez* shipwreck, in Prince William Sound, washed ashore along parts of the peninsula's Pacific coast, abruptly closing fisheries. In 1991, salmon fishermen refused to fish to protest low sockeye prices. In recent years, groundfish fisheries in the Gulf of Alaska and Bering Sea have brought new opportunities to small peninsula communities.

The business of fishing on the Alaska Peninsula draws people and financing from far beyond its shores. Local fishermen, both Natives and non-Natives, work alongside fishermen who come to the peninsula from elsewhere in the state and from outside Alaska, primarily the Seattle area. Financing for canneries, processing plants and some fishing vessels comes from foreign as well as domestic sources. The market also is international in scope. The drift gillnetter from Egegik may be affected as much by last year's glut of salmon in Japan or the strength of the yen against the dollar as by the current season's run of fish.

Then add the vagaries of nature. These fisheries depend on wild stocks traveling through vast regions of the North Pacific. Any number of unknowns affect the outcome of a particular season: changes in water temperatures, missing links in the marine food chain, pollution, indiscriminate fishing by high-seas trawlers, disease or flawed genetics carried to wild ocean stocks by foreign "farmed" fish. No one understands the ocean's complicated ecology.

The sea and its fish defy management. Yet all along its shores are people assigned to do just that. In Alaska, state and federal marine biologists try to keep fish populations steady and healthy. They analyze what appears to be happening, using science and personal observations. Using aerial surveys, fish tagging studies, tallies of fish entering spawning streams, daily trawl and pot surveys from fish buyers and fishermen, and past harvest and escapement records, they estimate current stocks and set harvest levels. Their ultimate goal is to keep fisheries from crashing.

The biologists determine when each fishery should start and end, opening and closing fisheries by emergency orders as the season progresses. They adhere to constraints established by politically appointed fishery managers. Fisheries of the Alaska Peninsula are under the jurisdiction of the Alaska Board of Fisheries, the North Pacific Fishery Management Council and the International Pacific Halibut Commission.

Harvests are allocated among different groups of fishermen, between different fishing districts, even between different types of seafood processors. While these allocations are predicated on biology and economics, they are inevitably influenced by politics. Often the politics of getting the fish to shore are just as important to the peninsula's fishermen as what goes on beneath the water's surface.

Yet despite all of this, hundreds of plucky individuals each year step into their boats and pit their wits against the currents of fortune in the time-honored occupation of fishing.

Only when the tide is high can skippers take their fishing boats, loaded with winter supplies, up the Chignik River into Chignik Lake. (Jane Barnett)

Salmon Fisheries of the Alaska Peninsula

Salmon are to the Alaska Peninsula what corn is to Iowa. The peninsula's rivers run flush with salmon. Of the five species caught on the peninsula, sockeye (red) salmon fetch the highest price per pound.

The peninsula's earliest people probably ate salmon as they traveled along the region's waterways. Throughout time, salmon became more culturally important as people gathered to fish the summer runs. Using nets and traps, they would catch enough salmon to last through the winter, drying the fish for food, trade and dog food.

The region's abundance of salmon was noted in 1778 by Capt. James Cook, as he sailed by during his search for the Northwest Passage. Yet the first foreigners to set foot on the peninsula came for furs, not fish. In the late 1700s, Russian American Co. fur traders arrived on the Alaska Peninsula and drafted Native men to hunt sea otters. The Russians established trading posts, first on the peninsula's south side at Katmai village in 1791, and later at the mouth of the Naknek River. The fur traders had little interest in salmon, other than drying small quantities for provisions.

After Russia sold Alaska to the United States in 1867, the Natives continued hunting sea otters and fur seals for the Americans, until the furbearers were practically exterminated.

Then the American salmon processors moved in. By the late 1880s, more than a half-dozen canneries and salteries operated on upper peninsula rivers emptying into Bristol Bay, including the Kvichak, Naknek and Ugashik. By 1897, the Bristol Bay canneries accounted for about 28 percent of all salmon coming out of Alaska.

Other early processors included a salmon saltery at Port Moller for a few years, and canneries at Orzinski Bay and Thin Point Cove on the lower peninsula around 1888.

The canneries imported Chinese, Japanese, Mexicans and Filipinos to work. Scandinavian fishermen first attracted by codfishing began gillnetting for salmon canneries around the peninsula. Unlike the transient cannery workers, many of the Scandinavians stayed, marrying into the existing mix of Russian and Native cultures.

Gradually, Natives began working for the canneries, although the canneries did not employ Natives in significant numbers until the labor shortage of World War II. This transition, along with epidemics, contributed to relocation and consolidation of various tribes. Native families moved closer to communities where commercial fishing opportunities existed, like Sand Point, King Cove, False Pass and Nelson Lagoon. Villages like Sanak, Unga, Belkofski, Squaw Harbor, Morzhovoi, Thin Point and Wosnesenski were abandoned.

RIGHT: Pete Blackwell holds a king salmon caught while commercial drift fishing. Chinook, or king, salmon are fourth in commercial value overall in the lower peninsula, but extremely important to fishermen in certain locales. Chinook is one of the two most important species at Port Heiden and are important to the economy of Nelson Lagoon. (Stuart Pechek)

LOWER RIGHT: Alaska Peninsula fisheries produce some of the highest quality sockeye salmon, such as these strips hanging in a Chignik smokehouse. Fishermen refer to sockeyes as reds, and are permitted to use only purse seines to catch the valuable fish. Japanese fish buyers years ago deemed Chignik sockeye as the world's best salmon for color, texture and oil content. This reputation accords Chignik sockeye a higher price per pound, although this price differential has slid in recent years with the worldwide glut of frozen salmon. (Jeff Caven)

Salmon boats come up to a tender anchored in the mouth of the Ugashik River. Tenders represent processing companies on the fishing grounds, and collect and deliver fish to processing plants. (Stuart Pechek)

The peninsula's salmon fisheries are some of the most productive in the state. In good years, a commercial salmon fisherman can gross upwards of $200,000 before crew and boat payments. Likewise, getting into the peninsula's fisheries doesn't come cheap. The state's limited entry salmon permits for the peninsula command premium prices. Asking price for a south peninsula set gillnet permit in fall 1993 was $150,000; drift gillnet permits averaged more than $400,000.

Local fishermen still hold a high percentage of permits in most peninsula fisheries, although the fleet includes more non-local and out-of-state fishermen than when the limited permit program was started in 1973. Also, the composition of fishing crews has changed in some places from being mostly family members to non-relatives willing to work for smaller shares of the catch.

The salmon fisheries of the Alaska Peninsula, while among some of the most commercially lucrative, are also some of the most controversial. Many of the fish caught off the Alaska Peninsula are simply passing through, headed for distant bays and rivers. Some are bound for Bristol Bay, others for the Yukon and Kuskokwim rivers, Cook Inlet, even Japan, Canada and Russia. "Fish are going in all directions. The board (of fisheries) tries to sort it out, to figure where all these fish are heading and who has the right to them. It's a giant, giant chess game," says Alan Quimby, state biologist in the Chignik salmon district.

Fishermen along Alaska's western and central coasts anxiously wait each season for their salmon to return, but Alaska Peninsula fishermen — by virtue of their location on the salmon migratory routes — get first chance. Off and on for years, Alaska Peninsula fishermen have been accused of catching too many fish destined for other places. Even on the peninsula, fishermen in neighboring river systems jealously watch the others' catches, crying foul if their own runs are late or low. Fishery managers limit peninsula harvests of sockeye and coho runs thought to be made up mostly of migrating fish, while targeting fishing on local stocks of sockeye, coho, pink and chum salmon. Peninsula fishermen say that their intercepts are only one of several factors possibly affecting upstream returns.

Here's a closer look at the Alaska Peninsula's salmon fisheries.

• The upper portion of the peninsula's south side that drains into Shelikof Strait — 150 miles of the peninsula from Cape Douglas to Kilokak Rocks at Imuya Bay — is part of the Kodiak salmon management area. This portion has 92 salmon streams: all produce pinks, half produce chums, nearly a third produce coho and six produce sockeye.

Commercial fishermen in this district use purse seines and beach seines. Fishing occurs June through October. The fish caught in this district are processed on Kodiak Island. There are no active towns or villages along this part of the peninsula, most of which is government property.

Several of the major runs through this area include migrating salmon. For instance, the salmon run in June past Cape Igvak, at the southern end of this district, is mostly made up of Chignik River sockeye. Cape Igvak fishermen are allowed to harvest only a portion of these Chignik-bound sockeye. In the north end of the district, the sockeye runs include Cook Inlet-bound fish.

This peninsula district is a small part of the much larger Kodiak area fishery. In 1991, the district brought in about $2.56 million, about 8 percent of the total $31.5 million Kodiak fishery.

This district's fishery is also smaller than others on the peninsula. More than half of the catch is pinks, which are smaller than other species and usually bring the lowest prices. For instance, fishermen in 1991 received about 36 cents for a 3-pound pink salmon compared to $4 for a 5-pound sockeye.

• The Chignik management area fishery spans 175 miles from Kilokak Rocks to Kupreanof Point. At the heart of the district are the villages of Chignik, Chignik Lagoon and Chignik Lake. Other villages include Perryville and Ivanof Bay.

The Chignik district is noted for sockeye salmon runs up the Chignik River system. From the bay, the salmon make their way up the Chignik River into Chignik Lake and above that, Black Lake.

The Chignik River also is the only known king salmon producer on the Pacific side of the entire Alaska Peninsula.

Chignik's commercial salmon fishery goes back to 1888, with the first pack of 13,000 fish. Between 1900 and 1924, 16 salmon traps operated here in wild abandon, hauling in some 1.3 million sockeye a year. Remarkably, the sockeye were not depleted by this. In 1922, the federal government installed a fish counting weir to make sure salmon made it into the river to spawn.

In 1955, the salmon industry-financed Fisheries Research Institute at the University of Washington started long-term research on Chignik sockeyes. They discovered that two runs with different life cycles entered the Chignik River. The early run spawns in Black Lake tributaries; the later run spawns in Chignik Lake. This knowledge drastically altered management of the fishery to allow escapement of both runs.

The Chignik fishery is further complicated by sockeye intercepts outside both ends of the district, north at Cape Igvak and south in the Southeastern District Mainland fishery, which includes Stepovak, Balboa and Beaver bays and which fishermen refer to as the Stepovak fishery. Management hinges on a complicated daily tally of harvests in the intercept and Chignik fisheries, as well as consideration of the number of salmon escaping into Chignik River to spawn. At least 600,000 sockeye must be harvested by Chignik fishermen before the intercept fisheries can start, and a schedule of escapement goals must be met through the season for fishing to continue. Biologists count fish passing through the weir for 20 minutes every hour, 14 hours a day, then extrapolate to come up with escapement.

In 1989, the year of the *Exxon Valdez* oil spill, Chignik fishermen were some of the few to fish on the peninsula's south side. The narrow outlet of the lagoon shut out oil moving along the coast. The fleet of salmon purse seiners, about 100 boats, worked inside the 175-square-acre lagoon, netting a modest $13.6 million in salmon.

In 1993, Chignik fishermen harvested more than 3.7 million salmon, the second strongest season on record in numbers of fish, said biologist Quimby. The largest harvest of nearly 4.44 million fish occurred in 1988. However, fishermen generally regarded 1993 as a poor year because of low prices. They got 80 cents a pound for sockeye compared to $1.75 a pound the year before. The low prices were offset somewhat by the larger harvest, but total earnings were still down considerably.

Now Chignik fishermen face a new challenge. Bristol Bay fishermen have complained to the state Board of Fisheries that too many of their coho are being taken in the Chignik sockeye fishery. Chignik fishermen say that their fishing is curtailed too much already by the Igvak and Stepovak intercepts, and they protest additional restrictions on behalf of western Alaska coho.

Two land-based processors in Chignik — Aleutian Dragon Fisheries and Chignik Pride

Crewmen from the F/V Sea Breeze *brail salmon in Chignik Bay. (Jeff Caven)*

powerful boat and skiff engines to increase fishing efficiency.

• The Area M fishery wraps around the end of the peninsula. It is the largest peninsula fishery in size, stretching 500 miles from Cape Menshikof, near Ugashik, to Unimak Pass then 375 miles back along the Pacific side to Kupreanof Point near Perryville. The south peninsula portion of this fishery has 185 salmon streams: sockeye are found in 23, pinks in 110, chum in 72 and coho in 57. The north peninsula portion contains 62 salmon streams: chinook are found in 10, sockeye in 32, pink in 11, chum in 38 and coho in 13.

Area M is the Grand Central Station of western Alaska salmon. Millions of fish migrate through these waters going in all directions. Managing these mixed stocks is an exhausting challenge, and to that end biologists segment Area M into two northern and four southern districts with 35 sections. Emergency fishery openings and closings punctuate the season. Fishermen stay tuned to the radio for fishery announcements like cats on the stalk, ready to pull in or throw out their nets when the orders come down.

Drift gillnetters and purse seiners catch the most fish, following the runs from the Shumagin Islands and Stepovak Bay during June and July, then around to the north side of the peninsula. There are almost 400 licensed fishermen that operate in Area M, with one of the highest rates of participation by resident Alaskans of any fishery in the state.

The catch from Area M waters accounted for 15 to 20 percent of the total salmon taken in Alaska in recent years, at an ex-vessel value between $31 million in 1991 and $85 million in 1988. The ex-vessel value of this fishery averaged about $42.6 million a year, 1979 through 1991.

Several major processing firms operate in the region, in addition to dozens of smaller ones. The Peter Pan cannery and seafood

ABOVE: Members of the Shugak family collect salmon from their setnets. The Shugaks fish the first four sites north of the Johnston Hill line southwest of Naknek. (Tom Shugak)

LEFT: Tender crewmen offload sockeye salmon to a processing plant. The fish are vacuumed out of the tender's hold. (Matt Johnson)

in the year-round mix to make ends meet.

About 80 percent of Chignik fishermen are local Natives, about 10 percent are non-Native Alaskans and the remainder are based Outside. Some of the local fishermen have winter homes in Anchorage, Kodiak and Seattle.

Stiff competition has brought changes to Chignik's purse seine fleet, as it has to other fleets on the peninsula. More fishermen are outfitting their boats with refrigerated seawater, to hold their catch in better condition and bring a few cents more a pound. Others are upgrading with more

Fisheries — handle most of the Chignik catch although floating processors moved into the bay during the height of the season. Aleutian Dragon processes cod, too, into early winter. Much of that cod is caught in pots and on longlines off seine boats; local fishermen go for cod after salmon season, another species

processing plant in King Cove is one of the largest anywhere. Sand Point has the largest boat harbor in the region and serves a number of floating processors, along with Trident's shore-based salmon and groundfish processing plant.

The major species produced in south peninsula streams are pink salmon, with chum salmon the second most important locally produced species. The south peninsula has numerous sockeye runs, though most are small. Thin Point and Middle Lagoon (Morzhovoi Bay) had substantial sockeye runs during the 1920s and 1930s, and in 1993 were producing sockeye at near historic levels.

A large part of the fishermen's earnings along the south peninsula come from harvesting migrant sockeye salmon. Fishing on the south side often takes place at the ends of prominent capes, where schools of passing salmon can include stocks bound for a dozen rivers hundreds of miles away. The south peninsula intercept fisheries include the South Unimak-Shumagin Islands (False Pass) June fishery, the Stepovak fishery and the cape fisheries of July and August where migrating cohos and sockeyes are caught.

The Stepovak fishery targets Chignik-bound sockeye during June and most of July, and those sockeye make up about 80 percent of the total harvest. After July, the Stepovak fishery targets local pinks, chums and coho.

For several decades the South Unimak-Shumagin Islands June fishery has been the most controversial intercept fishery in the state. This fishery, which dates back at least to 1911, commonly is known as the False Pass fishery because the catch used to be delivered to that community.

The June run is mostly Bristol Bay-bound sockeye. Since 1975, the state Board of Fisheries has allocated 8.3 percent of the preseason forecasted catch of the total Bristol Bay run to south peninsula commercial fishermen. Of that, 6.8 percent goes to South Unimak fishermen with the remaining 1.5 percent to Shumagin Islands fishermen.

Sometimes the peninsula fishermen's sockeye harvest gets cut short by inaccurate Bristol Bay preseason forecasts. For instance, record numbers of sockeye returned to Bristol Bay in 1992 and 1993, but the preseason forecasts fell millions of fish short. The peninsula fishermen caught their full allocation, but would have been allowed to catch even more had the forecasts been more accurate.

RIGHT: Using three-wheelers to haul gear and get around, setnetters near Naknek prepare to lay out their nets for another round in the salmon fishery. (Chlaus Lotscher)

BELOW: Salmon boats lie at anchor in the Naknek River waiting for fishing to open. For the decade 1983 through 1992, the annual average commercial sockeye salmon catch for the Kvichak-Naknek district was 10.6 million fish. (Chlaus Lotscher)

Chum salmon are also taken during this June fishery. In 1982, an unusually large harvest of 1.1 million chum, along with a failing fall Yukon River chum run, brought pressure from fishermen in the Yukon and Kuskokwim region to curtail or eliminate the June fishery. In the mid-1980s, the Board of Fisheries established additional restrictions on chum interception and set a cap of 400,000 chum. Peninsula fishermen

Fishing the Line

By Bob King

"Line fisheries" have become common in Bristol Bay and elsewhere in Alaska. Having evolved from the days when fishermen plied the bay in sailboats and fished the buoy lines, line fisheries became more prominent with establishment of limited entry fishing in the 1970s and with the increased costs of buying and operating fishing boats. Some of the newcomers "have less understanding of fishing etiquette," says Richard Russell, Alaska Department of Fish and Game commercial fish biologist in King Salmon and manager of the Egegik fishery. Line fisheries have their roots in competition, but the reality is much more aggressive.

At the beginning of a salmon fishing period, the fish and the fleet often tend to be fairly well dispersed throughout a district. But the fleet is so efficient these days that it can catch all the fish within the district in fairly short order, just an hour or two. After that, the action concentrates at the point where the salmon enter the district. For the Kvichak-Naknek district that's Johnston Hill on a flood tide and for the Egegik district it's the South line on a flood tide and the North line on an ebb tide.

Fishing along the lines can be exceptionally productive. When the run is strong, a single boat can catch hundreds of fish in just minutes. But heavily fished lines effectively cork off the run,

Fishermen deploy their nets along the Johnston Hill line where fish enter the Kvichak-Naknek district on a flood tide. (Tom Shugak)

catching most of the fish and allowing little for other drift and set fishermen. The practice has become controversial.

Line fisheries can degenerate from an orderly fishery into chaos, depending on the size of the run, the weather and the presence of public safety officers. In theory, a gillnetter will lay its net out along the district boundary line and drift inside the district with the tide, the operation being repeated over and over as sufficient space between the nets allows.

In reality, fishermen eager to get their nets wet will lay out just feet in front of other nets. To get to the front of the line, fishermen will run their boats over nets, often cutting them with their propellors. Some will ram other boats to intimidate smaller vessels or physically push them out of the way. Along the line, fishermen

often hurl insults and threats at one another from their flying bridges and occasionally guns are waved. Not all fishermen in a district fish the lines, some prefer to go pothole hunting, seeking out the holes where the fish rest; others with smaller boats perhaps, or less aggressive temperaments, fish away from the lines. Fishing the line also changes with the movement of the tides since fish swim with the tide and fishermen must follow the fish. Nonetheless, the boats of aggressive fishermen who routinely fish the lines carry telltale signs of the combat.

Though not all dents on fishing boats come from jostling along the line, the aluminum hulls of many line warriors in the Naknek and Egegik boat yard are dented and scraped, scars of fishing the lines. 1993 was a particularly frenzied fishing

season for sockeye in the Egegik district, which spans more than 40 square miles. In preseason forecasts, the Alaska Department of Fish and Game and University of Washington published reports predicting a good sockeye run, which attracted 1,045 boats, when 600 to 700 normally fish the run. And their efforts proved worthwhile because 21.8 million sockeye were caught in the Egegik district.

Some of the activity along the combative lines is illegal, but such fisheries have proved almost impossible to police with the current number of enforcement agents. The nature of the line fisheries sometimes encourages cheating. The district boundary line is established by regulation, usually on a loran line. Once the fleet has congregated along the boundary, it's obvious that the best fishing would be in front of that line. Line violations are endemic in Bristol Bay. Alaska Department of Public Safety officers cited hundreds of boats for fishing "over the line" (technically for fishing in closed waters) in 1993, mostly at Egegik. More than 70 boats were caught over the line during a single opening.

Fishermen who pleaded out to the charge received a standard fine of $3,000, plus forfeiture of their catch, often a like amount or more. Repeat offenders often got hit with much more severe penalties. Despite the stiff fines,

Jostling for position in tight quarters is just part of fishing on the lines, or boundaries, of the Egegik district in Bristol Bay. Lucrative fishing along the lines encourages frenzied activity such as cutting nets with propellors and pushing smaller boats out of the way. (Stuart Pechek)

many fishermen consider them simply a cost of doing business. Richard Russell says that based on a 62 cents per pound average weighted ex-vessel price, Bristol Bay fishermen, operating from 1,883 vessels, earned a minimum of $151.4 million just off the sockeye salmon run in 1993. These earnings do not include any post-season adjustments from the processors such as agreements for additional payment should the price of the fish increase, or

arrangements for boat storage, mechanics fees or meals at the canneries. In addition, some processors pay a loyalty bonus in the spring to ensure that certain fishermen will fish for them in the coming season. This enables the processors to claim a certain number of committed fishermen when they seek financing for their processing operations.

Line fisheries are in part the result of a changing economy in the business of fishing. A Bristol

Bay fishing permit now costs about $200,000. A fishing boat can often cost a like amount. Meanwhile, the growth of farmed salmon elsewhere and other factors have driven salmon prices down from a one-time-occurring high of $2.40 a pound for sockeye in 1988 to just 62 cents a pound in 1993.

The result is that fishermen with high debt loads have to be aggressive, and many have to fight the line, to survive.

ABOVE: *The Gregorio family fishes from the purse seiner* Antoinette Renae. *The Gregorios live on the "flat side" in Chignik Lagoon. Tony Gregorio has been fishing 32 of his 42 years. He has six children and the older ones work on the boat during the summer. (Jeff Caven)*

TOP RIGHT: *Born at Chignik Lagoon in 1919, Walter Stepanoff moved to Chignik Bay "when I was just a young guy." His father, William, was both a commercial fisherman and Russian Orthodox priest. A longtime fisherman, Walter remembers the family "lived off the country" when he was younger, though they used store-bought groceries to supplement their subsistence diet. (Mark Dolan)*

complained that in some years they would reach the chum cap before catching their full allocation of the more valuable sockeye. By 1992 the cap had risen to 700,000 chum, with conservation measures kicking in once 400,000 chum are harvested.

The issue of chum interceptions erupted again in 1993. Low chum returns triggered drastically curtailed commercial and subsistence chum fisheries on the Yukon and Kuskokwim rivers. Subsistence chum fishing on the Yukon was halted for the first time in history. Angry Native fishermen on those rivers, who depend heavily on chum for income and food, demanded that the state do something about south peninsula intercept fisheries.

Biologists would like to know the make-up of stocks in the intercept fisheries. A tagging study in 1987 traced these chum to Kotzebue Sound, Southeast Alaska, Japan and Russia, as well as the Yukon and Kuskokwim drainages. But it fell far short of offering definitive answers. Biologists are now looking for clues in fish scale patterns, genetic fingerprints similar to growth rings in trees, and in the differences in cellular proteins. Scale patterns and cellular proteins are distinctive to each river, and may pinpoint where the fish originate.

The south peninsula also has a post-June fishery focused on local stocks of pink, chum, sockeye and coho. But folks around the coast are now also claiming some of these sockeye and coho. Chignik, Kodiak and Cook Inlet fishermen say the sockeye are theirs, Bristol Bay and Yukon-Kuskokwim fishermen want the cohos, so another fight brews over intercept fisheries.

Around the tip of the peninsula to the northern coast are Area M's north peninsula fisheries. Most of the millions of Bristol Bay sockeye move well offshore of these fisheries although some mix with smaller runs of local sockeye. Bear River and Nelson Lagoon are the top two sockeye streams on the north peninsula. Chum salmon are usually the second most important north peninsula species, with major producers being Izembek and Moffet bays, Herendeen Bay and Port Moller, Bear River and Bechevin Bay. Coho outranks chum in importance in some years, with Nelson Lagoon being the largest producer.

For unknown reasons, the lower peninsula's north-side streams are not good pink salmon producers. Even streams that occasionally receive large numbers of spawning pinks fail to support good returns. Biologists think some feature in the marine environment limits pink salmon survival.

• Bristol Bay, the easternmost lobe of the Bering Sea, cuts into the northern base of the Alaska Peninsula. This shallow, often stormy bay is fed by six major river systems: the Togiak, Nushagak, Naknek, Kvichak, Egegik and Ugashik. Collectively, these rivers are home to the largest commercial sockeye salmon fishery in the world.

The northern Alaska Peninsula is part of the greater Bristol Bay basin. The Ugashik, Egegik, Kvichak and Naknek rivers drain the rolling lowlands of the upper peninsula west of the Aleutian Range into Bristol Bay. Huge tides, 20 feet and higher, push in and out of the rivers. The churning water carries tons of sediment that drop out to form muddy shoals at the rivers' mouths.

The salmon fisheries of the Ugashik, Egegik and Kvichak-Naknek river systems bring millions of dollars into northern peninsula communities. Sockeye are the most abundant and commercially important salmon, but chinook, chum, coho and pinks in even years contribute too. Pinks spawn when they're 2 years old and for some reason, the odd-year age class is practically non-existent in these rivers.

In 1992, the most recent year for which figures are available, these three districts accounted for more than $170 million, nearly 90 percent of Bristol Bay's total salmon harvest. About 30 processors handle the fish, shipping them out by air and sea as fresh, fresh frozen, canned and cured.

The Ugashik district includes Pilot Point on Ugashik Bay, and the hamlet of Ugashik upriver. The winding, 43-mile-long Ugashik River drains Upper and Lower Ugashik lakes. King Salmon and Dog Salmon rivers are also part of the Ugashik system. In recent years, the Ugashik district has bloomed, becoming the third most productive sockeye system in Bristol Bay.

The Egegik fishery took off during the early 1990s. This district in 1993 enjoyed a record sockeye harvest of 21.8 million fish, a quarter of all the sockeye harvested that year on the entire U.S. Pacific coast. The Egegik district historically is the second best sockeye producer in Bristol Bay. During the past decade, it moved into second place for coho production as well.

The Egegik district includes Egegik River, which drains Becharof Lake. This gravel-bottomed, clear lake — the second largest in Alaska — makes ideal salmon spawning grounds, although it can become quite rough when whipped by winds off the Bering Sea.

The King Salmon River, unconnected to the like-named river in the Ugashik district, also produces salmon in this district.

The granddaddy of all sockeye producers is the Kvichak-Naknek system, which includes the 50-mile-long Kvichak River that drains Lake Iliamna, Alaska's largest. Emptying into this lake is the Newhalen River out of Lake Clark. The Naknek River drains Naknek Lake and two others.

The Kvichak historically produces more sockeye salmon than any river in the world, with a record production in 1965 of 44 million fish, of which about half were harvested. Although its supremacy is currently challenged by the recent productivity of the Egegik, the Kvichak still produces amazing swarms of fish. For the decade ending 1982, Kvichak-Naknek's annual sockeye harvest averaged nearly 6 million fish. That annual average jumped to more than 10.6 million through 1992. Lined up end to end, that many salmon would stretch from Anchorage to Panama City.

This river system also produces significant numbers of chums and pinks.

Like elsewhere on the peninsula, these districts intercept each other's salmon to some degree. Scale pattern analyses indicate that about 70 percent of the Ugashik and Egegik catches are local stocks. The harvest of local salmon approaches 90 percent for the Kvichak-Naknek district. Kvichak set gillnetters have blamed their poor catches in

Breakers form when waves slosh up onto sandbars in Chignik Lagoon. Here the crew from the Louise A *fishes the breakers, an activity requiring much skill that becomes especially challenging when the wind is blowing from the southeast. Much of the fishing in this area is done in shallow water, a condition that has earned Chignik Lagoon quite a reputation in the fishing industry. (Jeff Caven)*

recent years on the Egegik's record harvests, although this hasn't necessarily been supported by scale pattern analyses, according to biologists.

Other Fisheries of the Alaska Peninsula

Many of the peninsula's salmon fishermen regear their vessels to fish for herring, cod, pollock, halibut, crab and other seafoods outside salmon season. Here's a look at some of the peninsula's other commercial fisheries.

• Pacific herring are small fish, 8 to 10 inches long. They are bony and oily, and are served whole as fresh, smoked, pickled, dry-salted or brine-cured. Herring roe and herring eggs on kelp are popular foods in Japan; processing plants in Alaska hire Japanese technicians to supervise roe preparation. Herring is also sold for bait to longline and pot fishermen.

Limited entry herring fisheries occur in 20 locations in Alaska, all regulated by the state Department of Fish and Game. Herring fisheries on the Alaska Peninsula include Port Heiden, Port Moller, Pavlov and Canoe bays, Shumagin Islands, Stepovak Bay and Shelikof Strait. Large herring fisheries occur at the top of the peninsula on each side, in the Togiak district of northern Bristol Bay and in Kamishak Bay of lower Cook Inlet. The Togiak district has the largest spawning population of herring in the eastern Bering Sea.

Herring sac roe fisheries are characteristically frenzied. Fishermen want to get the herring when they are fattest with roe but before they spawn. Purse seiners converge, waiting for the biologists surveying by air to give the word so they can drop their nets. Often these fisheries are over within minutes. In 1992, for instance, 301 purse seiners in the Togiak district netted 20,779 tons of herring — their entire catch for the year and 80 percent of the district's total harvest — in 20 minutes.

There are three commercial herring districts for the north side of the Alaska Peninsula: Port Heiden, Port Moller and Amak Island just west of Izembek Lagoon.

For years, vessels headed to the Togiak herring fishery scouted unsuccessfully for herring in Port Moller. Then in 1982, herring sac roe was successfully harvested off the peninsula's north shores. Most of the catch since has come from Port Moller and Herendeen Bay. In 1992, the total north peninsula herring harvest amounted to nearly 4,000 tons worth $1.17 million. Nearly two-thirds of that was pulled in from the Port Moller area with the balance from Port Heiden.

Off the peninsula's south side, herring concentrations are highest around the Shumagin Islands, and in Stepovak, Pavlov and Canoe bays. Canoe Bay has been the only consistent producer since 1986. This herring fishery is relatively small; the 1992 harvest of 180 tons brought an ex-vessel value of $78,150.

The south peninsula herring sac roe fishery has sputtered on and off since 1979. Landings were high in 1980 and 1981, but then the fishery closed for a few years to give the struggling food and bait fishery a chance to develop. That never happened; food and bait deliveries occurred here only in 1982 and 1991.

In the meantime, the winter food and bait herring fishery off the peninsula in northern Shelikof Strait is restricted to prevent over-harvest of Kamishak Bay stocks, which overwinter in this area. The northern Shelikof harvest cannot exceed 2 percent of the Kamishak Bay forecast.

• The Gulf of Alaska and the Bering Sea hold a dozen or so commercially valuable species of groundfish, including cod, pollock, mackerel, sole, flounder, rockfish and perch.

This fishery targets primarily cod and pollock, marketed as fillets and surimi, a protein-rich fish paste used widely in Japan and America. Pollock dominates in sheer numbers but cod is worth more, bringing 15 to 20 cents per pound to pollock's 6 to 9 cents per pound in 1993.

Because of its low price, pollock is a high-volume fish harvested mostly by large bottom trawlers that can haul 100 tons a run. The higher valued cod lives closer to shore, attracting the Alaska Peninsula's salmon seiners in the off season. Their 58-foot seine boats are generally too small for deep sea trawling, so many of them go after cod with pots and jigs. The exception to this are the salmon seiners from Sand Point who successfully trawl for pollock and cod around the Shumagin Islands and Sanak Island.

These fishermen are trawling in the same waters fished by their ancestors during the peninsula's original codfishery. Sand Point was founded as a local codfishing station and trading and supply post. Then later, during World War I, the closure of European codfisheries caused additional shore stations along the Alaska Peninsula to open, to handle the era's increased demand for Alaska cod.

Along with cod, pollock is becoming more important to the peninsula. Recent changes in federal management of groundfish fisheries are positioning Alaska Peninsula communities and local fishermen as players in the hot market for Bering Sea pollock. It is part of a change in the way the oceans are fished.

For the better part of this century, the seas off Alaska were dominated by foreign fishing fleets. Then Congress extended American ownership to 200 miles off shore. American fishing companies scrambled madly to replace the foreign boats. Rapid and unchecked growth ensued, albeit largely financed by displaced foreign interests.

Millions of dollars were poured into new trawlers, floating factory processors, and onshore processors. This created an insatiable demand for groundfish, particularly pollock, and pitted Alaska's shore-based processors against the Seattle-based factory trawler fleet in a race to harvest limited supplies.

In 1992, the North Pacific Fishery Management Council, amid heavy politicking from both sides, allocated almost all of the Gulf of Alaska pollock harvest and 35 percent of the Bering Sea harvest to shore-based processors. As part of the council's allocation, 7.5 percent of the yearly harvest through 1995 is reserved for Bering Sea coastal communities.

Ten Alaska Peninsula communities are among 55 Bering Sea coast towns in this program. The communities are represented by six regional associations in partnerships with American seafood processors to provide jobs and training to local residents. Port Heiden, Pilot Point, Ugashik, Egegik, Naknek, South Naknek, King Salmon and Savonoski belong to the Bristol Bay Economic Development Corporation in partnership with Oceantrawl Inc. The communities of Nelson Lagoon and False Pass are part of the smaller Aleutian-Pribilof Islands Community Development Association in partnership with Trident Seafoods Corp. and Aleutian Spray Fisheries.

• Some local fishermen longline for halibut on the south side of the peninsula and in Bristol Bay during the short commercial

TOP RIGHT: Willie Shugak, 72, mends a gill setnet at his family's site near the Johnston Hill line in Bristol Bay. (Tom Shugak)

RIGHT: Some salmon fishermen rig their boats to catch herring or other species when the salmon are out of season. These vessels fish for herring, which is sold for bait and whose eggs are in demand in Japan. (Stuart Pechek)

halibut openings. Most of the north side of the peninsula, where juvenile halibut congregate, is considered a halibut nursery and is closed to halibut fishing. Processors at Sand Point and King Cove buy halibut from local and transient fishermen, but disclosures of their tonnage are considered proprietary information and kept confidential by the International Pacific Halibut Commission.

• At one time, shellfish — king and Tanner crab and shrimp — played into the fishing economy of the peninsula. Today, however, these crab fisheries are closed on the peninsula and only a limited harvest of

Paul Entier weighs halibut at the Aleutian Dragon processing plant at Chignik Bay. Some local fishermen longline for halibut off the peninsula's south side, but waters on the north side are considered a halibut nursery and are closed to halibut fishing. (Jill Caven)

Dungeness crab occurs. Some Alaska Peninsula seafood processors still handle king and Tanner crab from ongoing fisheries in Bristol Bay and the Bering Sea.

Sand Point hosted one of the early king crab packing plants in the late 1920s, when a few daring salmon fishermen started exploring the crab fishery. In 1940, a Congressionally authorized study of king crab in Alaska, from Southeast through the Aleutians and into the Bering Sea, noted commercially viable populations on the south side of the Alaska Peninsula, particularly in Pavlov, Morzhovoi, Canoe and Cold bays. The fishery for red king crab opened in 1947.

During the booming years of this fishery in the mid-1960s, nearly half of the red king crab harvested came out of the Kodiak region, which included Shelikof Strait off the peninsula. The fishery peaked in western Alaska during the 1966-67 fishing season, with a total catch of just more than 180 million pounds. Of that, the lower Alaska Peninsula and Chignik areas contributed a record high 22.6 million pounds.

Red king crab harvests rapidly declined in the following years. Through the 1970s, the Alaska Peninsula king crab fishery averaged only about 3 million pounds annually and the Kodiak area average dropped to 15.8 million pounds a year. Meanwhile, crabbing vessels moved west into the Bering Sea. The once-lucrative fishery for red king crab off Kodiak and the Alaska Peninsula closed in 1983, leaving the commercial red king crab fishery to the western Aleutians, Bering Sea and Bristol Bay, where stocks are below historic levels, but enough to support modest harvests.

During the king crab decline, fishermen began selling the smaller Tanner crabs that they were catching in the king crab gear. As markets for Tanner crabs developed, Tanner gear became more specialized. By 1972, Tanner crab was a dominant winter and spring fishery.

Tanner crab harvests peaked in 1978 and 1979, at about 149 million pounds each year. The Alaska Peninsula and Chignik areas accounted for around 12 million pounds each year. The Kodiak area contributed more than twice that with the bulk coming from the Bering Sea. The Tanner fishery off the peninsula subsequently crashed and by 1990 was closed.

Only Dungeness crabs are harvested commercially now off the lower Alaska Peninsula. The peak Dungeness catch was 1.26 million pounds in 1968, the first year the fishery extended past the Kodiak area where it originated. The catch plunged drastically during the five years that followed and by 1973, no Dungeness were pulled from peninsula waters, outside Shelikof Strait in the Kodiak fishery.

By the mid-1970s, market demand and price increases renewed interest in Dungeness. The catch picked up in the Kodiak region, and a few boats returned to lower peninsula waters as well as moving westward into the Aleutians. The peninsula's peak harvest occurred in the 1983-84 season when 18 boats landed 1.2 million pounds, about a sixth of the total harvest that year, most of which came from Kodiak.

Dungeness fishing has since dropped off along the peninsula, to 80,000 pounds in 1991. Catch amounts since then are confidential because less than three boats have participated.

The trawl fishery for pink shrimp is another has-been fishery for the Alaska Peninsula. Trawling for pink shrimp commercially in western Alaska waters started in 1958, again in the Kodiak area including the northern peninsula waters of Shelikof Strait. After the Kodiak catch peaked with 82.2 million pounds in 1971, the trawlers moved into Chignik and lower peninsula waters.

The catch here peaked in 1977-78 with 71.5 million pounds, outdoing the Kodiak take and accounting for more than half the total catch. But two years later, commercial shrimp fishing ended off the lower Alaska Peninsula because of low stocks. Closure of the Chignik shrimp fishery soon followed.

Shrimp populations remain low, largely because these crustaceans are a favorite food of larger fish, particularly pollock that now occupy the sea in record numbers.

• A few developing fisheries off the Alaska Peninsula include ones for scallops, sea urchins and sea cucumbers.

Pacific Weathervane scallops are found in soft mud or sandy-gravelly ocean bottoms, 30 fathoms to 80 fathoms deep in the Gulf of Alaska and sporadically along the Alaska Peninsula.

In 1968, the first full year of scallop fishing in the Gulf, a fleet of converted crabbers, salmon seiners, halibut longliners and shrimp trawlers dropped steel mesh nets into the water for scallops. Crab mortality was an immediate concern. Scallop boats caught king crabs in their dredges, and about half of the crabs died before being thrown back. Concerns about dredger damage to crab stocks ended the scallop harvest along the lower Alaska Peninsula, from the tip of Unimak to Cape Kumlik.

In 1993, the state adopted a new management plan for scallops, giving the Kodiak district one of the largest allowable harvests in the state of 400,000 pounds; scallop beds in Shelikof Strait have been historic producers.

This plan opened a new area to scallop dredging off the Alaska Peninsula in the Bering Sea, about 30 miles north of Unimak Island. Scallops may be harvested here until the incidental catch of Tanner crabs reaches a set limit; the first scallop season in 1993 lasted two months. Eight scallop vessels participated. The boats carry crews to shuck the scallops, which are then iced or frozen. Most are shipped out of state.

Some interest has been shown in harvesting surf clams off the north coast of the peninsula. Surf clams are similar to razor clams, for which there was a commercial food

fishery until about 1975 on the peninsula's south side at Swikshak, Kukak and Hallo bays. In the mid-1970s, a food company worked with federal and state authorities to assess surf clam abundance in the Bering Sea, and one boat currently holds a yet-unused permit to do assessment work off the peninsula's north side.

Surf clams are an important food for walrus, and harvest of these clams would be subject to review. Also, surf clams are harvested by dredging with blasts of air and water, raising concerns about possible damage to crab habitats.

Divers have looked along the peninsula for sea cucumbers, which in recent years have been harvested commercially in small numbers around Kodiak Island. A few inquiries also have come in about sea urchins, but none have been commercially harvested

A crewman works in the hold filled with Dungeness crab caught near Mitrofania Island, east of Stepovak Bay. Limited fishing of Dungeness crab occurs in Alaska Peninsula waters; fishing is closed for king and Tanner crab. (Matt Johnson)

yet along the peninsula, said James A. Spalinger, state shellfish management biologist for Kodiak and the Alaska Peninsula.

Fishermen have occasionally plied Alaska Peninsula waters for snails, pot shrimp, squid, hair crab and octopus. There is a small market for the giant Pacific octopus, which is sometimes pulled aboard in trawls, pots and longlines during bottomfishing and crabbing. Frozen octopus is sold as halibut bait to longliners. Almost 22,000 pounds of octopus, of 158,800 pounds caught in western Alaska in 1991, came from the Alaska Peninsula.

The Bagoy saga continues...see page 86

Killer Whales: Wolves of the Sea

By Dan Strickland

Editor's note: *A commercial fisherman and writer, Dan knows the antics of killer whales firsthand.*

Their very name suggests a ferocious and cruel nature. Their appearance does little to still the perception; a stark dorsal fin 3 to 6 feet in height, a powerful streamlined body in sharp black and white relief reaching up to 30 feet and more, and a grin which reveals 50 strong white teeth. The image of a dangerous predator does not belie their ability either. Killer whales or orcas (*Orcinus orca*) are good at what they do.

On a June day in 1992 two men from Gustavus were rowing skiffs in the Icy Straits area of Southeast Alaska. They noticed two moose swimming toward the mainland, about a half mile apart and a half mile from shore. Suddenly a small pod of killer whales arrived, perhaps three or four animals. Though moose are not their typical fare, the opportunistic whales immediately attacked. One moose was summarily devoured, the other escaped in desperation into a kelp bed, only to ultimately drown in the

A matriarch (in rear) and her two adult sons from AB pod rest in Prince William Sound. Males have larger and usually straighter dorsal fins than females. (Eva Saulitis/North Gulf Oceanic Society)

entangling seaweed. From similar observations, with sea lions or porpoises more often the target, killer whales have acquired a fearful reputation. But there's another side to these enigmatic creatures, one which prompts the hopeful speculation that they are highly intelligent beings with whom we may one day communicate.

In April 1985 Todd Sylvester, a biologist at New Zealand's Leigh Marine Laboratory, was scuba diving off Goat Island. Upon surfacing he saw an orca about 30 feet away. Sylvester dove for

the bottom, though he did not feel particularly threatened. The orca followed, and as Sylvester glanced back the whale opened its jaws, sped up and gently closed them on his right foot. Sylvester pulled his foot out and swam a little harder. The whale kept pace, and with a swift move took Sylvester's left leg in its mouth, this time up to his calf. Sylvester turned on his back and kicked his leg out with some urgency. The killer whale mouthed Sylvester several more times before leaving him unscathed, if a bit shaken.

Two more incidents of killer whales harmlessly "gumming" divers were reported off the New Zealand coast, as well as several encounters where the whales were close, and curious. One large pod of 35 whales (whom researchers have dubbed AB pod) in Prince William Sound was noticeably tolerant of fishing boats and observers. Ironically, as we shall see, this easy familiarity may have helped lead these particular animals into serious trouble.

Killer whales are found throughout the world oceans, from Antarctica to the north polar cap. They prefer coastal or continental shelf waters, and favor cool or cold ocean temperatures. Estimates of killer whale numbers are given only grudgingly, and usually with a caution as to the inaccuracies inherent in any assessment of marine mammal numbers. Cruises in Antarctic waters yielded a guess of 70,000 orcas, while surveys of the North Atlantic produced a figure of 6,600 killer whales from that region.

In Alaska killer whales are found in coastal waters from Southeast to the Gulf of Alaska, from Prince William Sound to Kodiak Island and Shelikof Strait, along both sides of the Alaska Peninsula and the Aleutian Islands, and north into the Bering, Chukchi and Beaufort seas. A few of the whales of these polar seas have been seen pushing north as the ice recedes in summer, and then moving south as winter approaches and the pack ice advances.

The National Marine Fisheries Service (NMFS) did a survey in 1992, which estimates the number of whales in Southeast as 183, the number calling Prince William Sound home as 350, and the number for the southeast Bering Sea, central and eastern Aleutians, south of the Alaska Peninsula and in waters off Kodiak as 182. These numbers

are undoubtedly conservative, but they are the best we have to go on at present.

"Home" is perhaps a misnomer for these wide-ranging animals, yet two distinct types of whales have been identified by scientists. One group is transient, while another is resident. We must define these terms carefully, however, for the characteristics of each group are somewhat different from the usual connotations of these labels.

Two species of killer whales were originally described: *Orcinus orca* in the Atlantic Ocean and *Orcinus rectipinna* as its Pacific Ocean counterpart. Other species have been proposed from time to time, such as a glacial whale and a dwarf killer whale from Antarctica, but presently the

killer whale, largest member of the dolphin family, is considered to be a single variable species worldwide.

Males can reach 32 feet and weigh in at 9 or 10 tons. Females grow up to 28 feet and tip the scales at 5 or 6 tons. Males are distinguished by their larger dorsal fin, which can rise to 6 feet, while those of females are about half that size.

Resident whales are seen frequently in a particular region, at least in the summer, eat primarily fish, have larger pods than transients, and tend to travel along the coast in midpassages and off the coast. If they do venture close to the coastline, they tend to travel from headland to headland. Transients are seen less frequently. They prey

upon marine mammals, travel in smaller pods and usually investigate bays and bights more closely than would residents. Transients also vocalize less often than residents, and have sharper points on their dorsal fins than do resident whales, who sport more rounded tips.

Killer whale society, like that of lions and elephants, is matriarchal or centered around the females. Pods are defined as the largest cohesive group of individuals that travel together most of the time. They are essentially family groups clustered around the mother, both literally and figuratively; the swimming formations have the calves closest to their mothers. Next in proximity are the adult sons, with adult daughters farther out, surrounded in turn by their offspring.

Though societies formed around females or extended families are not rare (wolves and hyenas also do this), what is unique about the social fabric of killer whales is that the adult males do not disperse. In 17 years of research in Southeast Alaska and the Pacific Northwest no whale has been observed to change pods, at least among residents. Transients apparently have a slightly different social structure, and some whales may disperse when they reach adulthood. Resident pods then, and groups of pods known as communities, are essentially large extended families. There are four identifiable pods in

A killer whale from transient pod AT attacks an adult Dall's porpoise in Prince William Sound. It took four whales 40 minutes to kill this porpoise. Porpoises can swim fast, but the whales isolated this animal from a group of porpoises and kept attacking it until the porpoise became tired and confused. When it tried to rest, the whales rammed it from underneath, propelling both themselves and the porpoise into the air. (Eva Saulitis/ North Gulf Oceanic Society)

LEFT: *Killer whales have good vision. They can't see far under water because plankton frequently obscures the water. To aid them when trying to see above water, they spy-hop, holding themselves vertical in the water while they look at something of interest such as a boat, rocks or other animals. They may locate prey this way, but scientists speculate that killer whales are more likely to listen for movement and splashing in the water to find prey. (Eva Saulitis/North Gulf Oceanic Society)*

ABOVE: *A multipod group of more than 100 killer whales rests near the surface in Prince William Sound. Resident pods come together in late summer and fall as an aspect of social behavior. Pods from Southeast and Kodiak have been seen mixing with Prince William Sound pods. Males sometimes leave their mother to temporarily congregate with males from other pods, females also exhibit this behavior.(Craig O. Matkin/North Gulf Oceanic Society)*

Southeast Alaska, nine in Prince William Sound. There has been insufficient research in other areas of Alaska to determine pod numbers.

Killer whales are long-lived animals. Pods grow slowly, and communities may contain animals reaching across four generations. Female orcas reach sexual maturity when they are about 15 years old. They typically produce four or five calves during a 40-year span, carrying each calf for 17 months and usually giving birth between fall and spring. Females can survive to 80 or 90 years. Males reach sexual maturity in 18 to 20 years, and exhibiting the usual male/female pattern found in the animal kingdom, survive to a fewer 50 or 60 years. With a relatively low reproductive rate,

fewer than 3 percent per year, killer whale communities may, in a sense, be centuries old.

Each pod speaks its own language too, or at least is thought to have a pod-specific dialect. Killer whales produce ultrasonic clicks, as do other dolphins, which have been shown from studies of captive animals to be primarily for echolocation. The fleshy bulge on top of the whale's head (the melon), focuses these high-frequency sound waves into a cone-shaped beam directed ahead of the swimming animals. Orcas also whistle and squeak in complex patterns, which are thought to be mostly social signaling. Sound waves are received through the whale's jawbone (the ear canal is closed) and are conducted directly to the inner ear. This anatomical arrange-

ment imparts a remarkable sensitivity to their hearing. Prince William Sound's AB pod picked up the sound of

fishermen hauling longlines from seven miles away. And being the intelligent, opportunistic predators that they are, the whales began to equate these noises with the proverbial free lunch.

Since 1985 blackcod and halibut fishermen in Prince William Sound have reported devastating losses by killer whales. Bering Sea fishermen suffered whale attacks a year earlier, but the problem escalated about the same time Prince William Sound's AB pod began targeting longliners.

The orcas arrive shortly after the fishermen commence hauling their gear aboard. In what has been described as cowboy and Indian fashion the whales circle the boat, then dive down and nip the struggling fish neatly off the hooks. They can completely strip the gear, often leaving nothing but fish lips.

"They have incredible finesse," marvelled Jack Knutsen, skipper of the *Grant* and veteran Bering Sea fisherman. "There's no tug like when a sea lion pulls a fish off. The line just comes up empty." He shook his head, "You'd think with such a big animal you'd feel *something*!"

Conflict between killer whales and fishermen is nothing new. Norwegian halibut fishermen have long complained of losses. Trevella fishermen in South Australia were nearly put out of business in the late 1970s by whale depredations, and Japanese skippers hauling tuna from the Indian Ocean reported killer whales stealing fish from their lines.

The problem came home to roost for Alaskans as fishermen began to target blackcod more heavily. Foreign fleets from Korea, East Germany and Poland had been fishing blackcod in Alaska waters since the early 1970s. Japanese and Soviet boats had been longlining and gill-netting these waters since the 1950s. With this intense effort, blackcod stocks at last began to plummet. Passage of the Magnuson Fishery Conservation and Management Act in 1976 banned foreign vessels from the Pacific coast and put them under quota off Alaska. With the low numbers of blackcod came a corresponding rise in price to fishermen, and the stage was set for local fleets to turn to a fishery most had previously neglected. Since 1977 blackcod stocks have rebounded, creating further opportunity for a viable fishery. In the Bering Sea and Prince William Sound, longline effort for blackcod sharply increased. In 1986 Prince William Sound fishermen caught close to 160,000 pounds of fish, while out west longliners harvested more than 8 million pounds.

The hardest hit area in the Bering Sea for killer whale interactions is just north of Akutan Pass, although this region sees the heaviest fishing as well. The impacts are serious, both financially and relative to the fishery's management. Rick Steiner, with the University of Alaska's Marine Advisory Program, traveled to Dutch Harbor in 1987 to interview longline skippers and crew.

Steiner estimated the fishermen were losing *at least* $1 million worth of fish per year. And the amount of fish the whales were taking — anywhere from half to double what the fishermen landed — was not being counted against the harvest quota, giving rise to concerns from a management perspective. Fishermen were quick to retaliate against the orcas, but the whales have proved difficult, if not impossible, to dissuade.

Ken Adams, a longliner from Prince William Sound, experimented with seal bombs, large waterproof firecrackers designed to frighten seals and sea lions away from fishing gear.

"At first they didn't work at all," he recalled. "Then I weighted them so they would sink, and positioned one of my crew up on the bridge. From there he could shoot them out a hundred yards with a slingshot." Adams shrugged, adding "It seemed to work about 80 percent of the time, but we had to keep him up there slinging seal bombs for the whole set. We'll have to see whether it continues to work or not, I guess."

Seal bombs and other acoustical harassment devices used to keep marine mammals away from salmon hatcheries have ultimately proved useless. Japanese bang pipes, a 15-foot metal rod with a 2-foot bell attached to one end, which are lowered into the water and struck repeatedly, have been used to herd dolphins, but are also ineffective against orcas.

"The only recourse I've found that works," sighed Mark Lundsten, Bering Sea fisherman, "is to quit fishing. Or at least run to marginal fishing grounds where the whales are less interested. If you're in good fishing," he claimed, "the whales can take 100 percent of the fish. When it comes to cleaning the gear...they're really good." One fisherman from the Bering Sea estimated his season's loss at between 100,000 and 200,000 pounds of fish.

Jack Knutsen marvelled at the whales' adaptability. "We tried fishing cooperatively, where one boat starts hauling gear, and then when the whales show up the skipper drops his gear back down and radios another captain to begin hauling. The whales ran from one boat to the other for a while," he recalled, "but then they split into two groups and cleaned us both out."

"I wish somebody *would*

A killer whale mother and calf swim near Chignik Bay. A 1992 survey of killer whale numbers counted 182 animals in waters off Kodiak, the Alaska Peninsula, the central and eastern Aleutians and the southeast Bering Sea. (Jeff Caven)

This subgroup of resident killer whales, or orcas, display two different saddle patch shapes on their dorsal surface. These differences allow researchers to identify individual whales. (Eva Saulitis/North Gulf Oceanic Society)

discover a way to communicate with killer whales," he grinned. "I'd like to be able to talk this over with them; *Here, you take the turbot and leave me the cod.*"

Orcas might negotiate; they *are* specific about what they target. They like blackcod and halibut, but turn their melons up at rockfish, flounder, dogfish and other species less profitable to fishermen.

Dynamite was tried as frustrated skippers escalated their efforts to win back their fishery, but even high explosives failed to deter the killer whales for long. Greenpeace became concerned about the rising violence, and lobbied successfully for a modification of the Marine Mammal Protection Act. As the Act originally read, fishermen could request a permit allowing them to harass or kill whales to protect their catch. After Greenpeace's effort the whales could be mildly harassed, but not killed. One other kind of violence beyond the use of explosives had also prompted Greenpeace to intervene...reports of fishermen shooting killer whales with high-powered rifles.

Craig Matkin has studied the orcas of Prince William Sound since 1977. By 1984, using techniques developed in British Columbia by the late Dr. Michael Bigg, Matkin and his associates had photographed and identified more than 300 different killer whales in the sound, comprising nine resident pods and four transient groups. In 1985, eight of these whales, all belonging to AB pod, showed circular white marks diagnostic of bullet wounds. Another five whales showed wounds that could possibly be attributed to bullets.

Between 1985 and 1986 six whales were lost from AB pod. This was an unprecedented 7 percent mortality figure, where 2 percent or less is the norm. Other pods in Prince William Sound were unaffected. Matkin and Steiner had determined that the AB pod was the only one involved with the blackcod fishery. Matkin called Steve Zimmerman, of the National Marine Fisheries Service, at his home one night and alerted him to the problem.

With the subsequent pressure brought to bear from Greenpeace, the Sierra Club, local recreational groups and fishermen's organizations as well, the shootings seemed to have stopped. Greenpeace circulated a poster exhorting fishermen to "Share the waters with orcas... share your ideas with us," and when killer whales were around to "Keep your cool above deck and your guns below." Fishermen realized that shooting did little to keep the whales away, while it did infinite harm to themselves in the public's perception.

Mortality rates declined, and AB pod rebounded with a phenomenal five calves in 1988, putting the number of whales in the pod at 36.

Then an even greater tragedy befell the whales. On March 24, 1989, the *Exxon Valdez* ground her bow on Bligh Reef and gushed 11 million gallons of crude oil into the sound's clear waters. Six days later AB pod was sighted swimming slowly though heavy oil sheens. Seven whales were missing. By 1990, six more whales were gone. Thirteen whales killed; a nearly 20 percent mortality figure for *both* 1989 and 1990. This was unheard of in killer whale research anywhere. The sound's other pods, fortunately, seemed to have avoided the oil.

In 1992 two calves were born into AB pod, and another arrived in 1993. Matkin, and others with the North Gulf Oceanic Society, are attempting to set up permanent hydrophones in the sound. With these in place they could more accurately track the movements of resident pods. Photo-identification work will continue, its worth proven both by the documentation of mortalities following the *Exxon Valdez* incident and the fishermen/orca controversy. Indeed a 1992 survey from the Gulf of Alaska and the Bering Sea reported nine killer whales with evidence of possible bullet wounds so the need for ongoing research throughout Alaska waters is paramount.

Editor's note: *A former Sitka resident, Lyn works in the medical field when she is not writing about life in Southeast.*

A crowd gathers on the gravel road leading up to the Alaska Raptor Rehabilitation Center, cameras and videorecorders in hand. People appear on the grassy bluff above, several of them clothed in heavy leather jackets and gloves. A woman holds a bald eagle in her arms, her head and eyes covered with a leather hood. For the past four months, the eagle has been known as Cascade, an identity she is about to leave behind.

Another handler loosens the leather strings securing the eagle's hood, then waves to the waiting crowd below.

Eyes on the eagle, the crowd begins to count: "One, two." On "three" the hood is swiftly removed, and the handler lifts her arms away from the bird, rolling it forward. A few quick strokes of the strong wings, and the eagle sails over the crowd, down over the steep hillside thick with spruce, alder and hemlock, across the choppy, gray water of Sitka Sound and into the forest beyond.

This moment of triumph is the end of a story that had its dismal beginning on a damp, chilly February day. The bird was found perched on a log on the beach, facing the sunset. Technicians examined her and discovered that she was weak and emaciated. The eagle had

Raptor Recovery a Passion in Sitka

By Lyn Kidder

Rehabilitation technician and trainer Scott Ford shows off Buddy, a 5-year-old eagle that has imprinted on humans. Buddy displays adult plumage, his head is almost completely white and his eyes and beak are yellow. Immature eagles have dark feathers, eyes and beaks; successive molts give them a mottled dark brown and white plumage. (Frederic Moras)

recently gorged on something, and was suffering from "crop statis," a condition in which food is unable to pass from the crop. Evacuating the crop discharged the remains of a road-killed cat. Rehydrated with intravenous (IV) fluids, the eagle was given the name Cascade and placed in the critical care area.

The critical care unit of the clinic is a series of large kennels, each holding an injured bird. Much of the clinic's equipment looks similar to that used for humans, and in fact much of it is donated by hospitals. X-rays, IVs, injections, daily weighings, bandage changing are all noted on the patient's chart. When the patient has recovered sufficiently, it is put in a mew, a large, outdoor flight cage that provides room to fly from perch to perch, allowing the birds to exercise and recover.

Most of the injuries are from collisions with civilization, in the form of motor vehicles, power lines, traps and guns. "We offer balance," said Dick Griffin, center director. "We are balancing Man's actions. We're offering a second chance to birds who have had negative experiences with something that Man has done — a power line, or trap or a landfill. That doesn't mean that we want to get rid of power lines, traps or landfills. We'd like to educate and work with power line engineers, trappers and landfill operators to prevent injuries."

The Alaska Raptor Rehabilitation Center was founded in 1980 with a three-fold mission: the care of injured raptors, or birds of prey; education and research. The center treats approximately 80 birds a year, the majority of which are American bald eagles, although no injured bird is refused treatment and the center has cared for everything from a hummingbird to a trumpeter swan. Of the birds that come to the center, 70 percent are saved. Forty percent are returned to the wild, the remaining 30 percent, whose injuries prevent them from surviving in the wild, are sent to zoos and captive breeding programs. The center considers only those sites and programs that are capable of providing long-term care because bald eagles can live to age 50 in captivity.

The bald eagle population of Alaska is estimated to be 40,000, the largest concentration in the United States. The bird that is the country's national symbol is considered endangered in the contiguous states because of habitat loss and use of pesticides

LEFT: *Between 12,000 and 15,000 visitors tour the Alaska Raptor Rehabilitation Center annually, many of them from cruise ships traveling Alaska's Inside Passage. The center receives no federal or state funding; its operations are supported by donations. (Frederic Moras)*

LOWER LEFT: *Tracy Harris holds Clicker, a western screech owl. Owls are also raptors, birds of prey that kill with their talons. The Alaska Raptor Rehabilitation Center has several owls whose injuries make them unsuitable for release into the wild. These educational birds help with programs to increase knowledge of raptors. (Frederic Moras)*

LOWER RIGHT: *Eagles feed on salmon in a mew, a large, outdoor flight cage. All the fish is donated by fishermen and local fish processing plants. Salmon heads are a favorite. Buffy, right, is an immature eagle, about 3 years old. (Frederic Moras)*

such as the now-banned DDT.

"The birds that we treat and release do not make a big difference in the eagle population in Alaska," said Elaine Craddick-Patt, educational program director. "We do make a big difference when we send a bird down south in a captive breeding program. But truly, the job of this organization, more than anything, is education. We need to teach everyone — not just kids — how to prevent the injuries in the first place, and when and how to intervene and help an injured bird." The center has worked with a Sitka third-grade class to produce a video-tape teaching children not to rush to rescue a baby bird whose parents may be close by. The education department supplies video and printed materials to elementary schools, but the most popular program is an "in-eagle" visit from Buddy.

Buddy is an unusual case because his injury is not physical. He was found in Kake, a small community southeast of Sitka. Only a few months old, but already the size of a full-grown eagle, he hung around the village, scavenging and living on handouts. He became a popular local character, and one resident gave him the name Rosebud, not knowing that he was a male.

One day at the playground, the eagle spied a bright red ball in a child's hand. Raptors can see color, and red is the color of salmon meat, the bald eagle's chief food. Buddy tried to grab it for a closer look, frightening the child badly, and the local police arrested Buddy.

The bird was shipped via Alaska Airlines, which provides free transport for injured birds, to the raptor center, examined and found to be physically sound. Like other eagles, he was placed in the mew for observation. But there was something unusual in Buddy's response. Instead of immediately flying away from the humans and joining the eagles on the perch, Buddy cowered close to the humans and appeared afraid of the other eagles. Clearly, Buddy had an identity problem.

"When Buddy was several weeks old, he was probably picked up and raised by people,"

TOP RIGHT: Rebecca May, rehabilitation manager, exercises an adult eagle. Leather straps, or jesses, are attached to the bird's ankles, and a series of cables allows the bird to fly up to 50 yards. Evaluation of flying ability is essential before release. (Frederic Moras)

RIGHT: The Alaska Raptor Rehabilitation Center focuses on birds of prey, collectively called raptors. One of Alaska's more striking species of raptor is the gyrfalcon, largest of the state's falcons. (John Sarvis)

explained Rebecca May, rehabilitation coordinator. "There's a certain window of time when a bird imprints on its parents. The eyes focus, they see the parent, the one that is feeding them and the chick says, 'Okay, this is my species, this is who feeds me so this is who I should associate with and who I should seek as a mate.'"

Buddy is now 5, the age of maturity in bald eagles. His nesting instinct is beginning to emerge, but he wants to make a nest with humans. His trainers oblige him by bringing sticks and helping him build his nest. His favorite companion is Scott Ford, rehabilitation technician and Buddy's chief trainer.

"I have a different connection with him than most people have, and it's really sad (that he can never be released). He doesn't seem to notice the difference, but he likes to go out and fly, and I wish that he could be out there with the other eagles."

Scott and Buddy travel to elementary schools in Alaska and the western states, with the hope that seeing a bald eagle up close will foster appreciation and concern for wildlife. It is that concern and compassion that makes the existence of the Alaska Raptor Rehabilitation Center possible. Center board member Liz Beechwood perhaps said it best: "It's helping a fellow creature to survive who might not make it on its own that drives all our volunteers."

The Flowering of Anchorage

By Richard P. Emanuel

Editor's note: *In* Alaska's Bears, *Volume 20, Number 4, Dick Emanuel described the Bagoy family's exploits throughout Alaska before they moved to Anchorage. This article completes the Bagoy saga, with a look at one of Anchorage's pioneer families.*

In 1921, John Bagoy had ridden out another gold boom. He and his wife, Marie, had joined the stampede to Iditarod in 1910. John had dug gold in the Klondike and prospected in Nome and California. He and Marie had sought their fortune in Nevada and in Fairbanks. They had rushed to Iditarod with a 2-year-old son in tow, and had stayed long enough to produce four daughters.

John's gold fever had been in remission during most of his time in Iditarod. The Bagoys had run three roadhouses, then

taken up vegetable farming and greenhouse gardening in Flat, on Otter Creek near Iditarod. But 11 years after the boom, the area was in decline. It was time for one last move.

In August 1921, the exodus began. John and Marie Bagoy and their five children, ages 2

to 13, left the farm in Flat. Peter Bagoy , now 86, was the oldest child. At age 13, he was older than Anchorage, their boomtown destination.

Peter recalls their journey. "The family left Flat with two trunks, two barrels and two suitcases," plus a handful of

Marie Bagoy tends flowers on her back porch about 1939 or 1940. Marie sold the flowers from the front part of her house, which her husband, John, built in 1935. Marie had the living room converted into a display area with coolers for the flowers and a counter with a cash register. (Courtesy of the Bagoy family)

other bags. Transport was first aboard a flatbed Model T truck, mounted on wooden rails. At five mph, it took nearly an hour and a half to reach the Iditarod River, where they boarded a gasoline-powered launch, the 36-foot *Sea Wolf*. "For two days, the diet was hotcakes," Peter recalls. Wooden benches served as tables, seats and beds.

For the voyage through mosquito-infested Shageluk Slough, they transferred to the *Saint Joseph*, a sternwheeler from the Jesuit mission in Holy Cross. A day and a half later, they swept onto the Yukon River and docked at Holy Cross to await a steamboat upriver. "There were no accommodations for travelers at Holy Cross, but the Natives were kind and offered an empty cabin," Peter says. They also generously shared with the family "ducks, geese, fish and Indian ice cream."

After a week, the SS *Seattle III* arrived and the Bagoys sailed up the Yukon in style. "There were staterooms, a large dining room and a social room where one could read, play cards or dance to an old Edison phonograph," Peter says. "The SS *Seattle III* made 20 miles a day, stopping to load wood along the way. Passengers and crew pitched in

together to load the wood. Once in a while the boat ran aground in shallow water or hit a sand bar and it took hours before it was free again."

In Fort Gibbon, near present-day Tanana, the Bagoys left the Yukon and proceeded up the Tanana River aboard the *General Jacobs*. Two and a half weeks out of Holy Cross, 30 days after they left Flat, the family gained Nenana, ready for the last leg of their journey. Nenana was a railroad town of 600 people in 1921. It lay 300 miles by rail from Anchorage. But there was a catch: Only about 250 miles of track had been laid.

"Father's money was running out fast and winter was coming

on," Peter remembers. After two weeks, Bagoy paid a teamster $300 to take the family across the railroad gap, south of Healy. First, they rode a work-train 54 miles south to the Healy construction camp. Then a flatcar loaded with lumber took them the final 10 miles to the end of the track. They spent the night in a leaky barn two miles north of McKinley Park and set out in the morning with the teamster, Marie and the four girls riding the wagon while John and Peter slogged on foot and forded streams along the muddy railroad grade.

"Where the bridges were not finished," Peter recalls, "the wagon bounced and swayed

and wallowed up steep inclines through the Nenana canyon, frightening the children. One barrel was not properly secured and slid off the wagon, going over a 300-foot drop into the river." The barrel held all of Marie's mementos from Europe, including her wedding dress.

In places, the road was so dangerous that Marie and the girls got down and trudged through the mud with the men. On the second day, it snowed as they neared Cantwell. The third day, they reached the tracks in Broad Pass, where they boarded a train headed south.

The ride to Anchorage seemed luxurious in upholstered seats, with a pot-bellied, coal-burning stove in each car. Half of one car was a diner, offering potato chips, candy, fresh fruit and other treats. The train rolled south at 20 mph most of the time, according to Peter. "The grade was soft, causing the coaches to uncouple from the engines at times."

The Bagoys arrived in Anchorage on Oct. 5, 1921. It was a cold day but the ground was bare. Early Anchorage was built on the south side of Ship Creek, on a bluff above the rail station. It was a railroad construction town, built after the federal government selected a route for the Alaska Railroad, in 1915. From a handful of homesteaders, the town grew to more than 6,000 people at the peak of construction, in 1917. Three years later, the railroad's southern

Snow and Christmas lights bedeck the Bagoy shop and home at Christmas, 1942. The FTD florist symbol adorns the door. (Courtesy of the Bagoy family)

About 1965 Marie Bagoy and her children gather for a family photo. From left are Mary, Gabrielle, Peter, Marie, John, Doris and Eileen. (Courtesy of the Bagoy family)

segment was done and the population fell to 2,000 to 3,000.

After living in temporary quarters in a shack on the west side of town, John Bagoy found a permanent home for his family in two shingled buildings at the corner of Fourth Avenue and A Street. "The family slept in one house and used the other for cooking and living," Peter recalls. "It was very hard at first. Mother cried a lot and wanted to go back to Flat." The children lacked immunity to a host of new diseases, "and immediately became ill with flu, chicken pox, measles" and other maladies.

Despite setbacks, the Bagoys threw themselves into their new life with typical optimism and vigor. John signed on with the Alaska Railroad and in his spare time, moved his two houses together and added a bedroom.

In the summer, he built a greenhouse and raised vegetables and starter plants for sale. They grew tomatoes, cucumbers, radishes, onions. And of course, Peter says, "Mother always had her flowers."

They cleared more land to raise crops for their own table and for sale. Bagoy acquired an old locomotive boiler and used it to heat his greenhouse. He fired up the boiler in spring, starting in March, to jump-start the growing season. He heated again in fall, until mid-September. The Bagoys were, for many years, the sole commercial source of fresh produce in Anchorage.

In June 1922, the couple's eighth and last child was born. John was their sixth surviving baby and their second surviving son. Now 71, he recalls his early Anchorage youth.

The commercial district ran along Fourth Avenue, John recalls, from about C to I Streets. "Everything seemed to stay on Fourth Avenue. E Street was about the center of town." The Empress Theater, a large cinema, was a landmark at Fourth and G. To the east, "Fourth Avenue went as far as Eagle Street, and there was a dairy farm at the end of the street." Peter Bagoy used to herd cows for the farmer, Fred Petersen, to earn spending money.

There was a red-light district, first on Ninth Avenue, later along C Street, where prostitutes served railroad roughnecks and visiting hardrock gold miners. "These girls were the backbone of the community, because if it wasn't for them, I don't think half the business people in town would have survived," says John. "They were the best customers my folks had for tomatoes, fresh vegetables, flowers — they bought the best. When I was in high school, I used to deliver groceries for various stores in town. They were always the best customers. And they always paid cash, silver dollars."

Ninth Avenue marked the extreme southern edge of town through the 1930s. Today's "parkstrip," named Delaney Park after an early mayor, was cleared as a firebreak, in 1923. It served

as a nine-hole golf course and as a landing strip for bush pilots, especially when Merrill Field, built in 1930, was too muddy. Like many early Anchorage lads, young John's first airplane ride took off from the parkstrip.

Like their parents, kids in early Anchorage were a pretty hard-working lot, recalls John. Besides odd jobs like delivering groceries, "Ship Creek was the big thing for us in the summertime," he says. "Salmon ran so thick you could kick them out of the water. There was a fellow on Third Avenue who would give us kids a nickel apiece for humpies, and we'd go down and gaff them out of the water, put them in a gunnysack and carry them up the hill." Older children worked in canneries in the summer, or dug sewer and water lines or joined railroad crews.

"In wintertime, we'd skate on ponds around town, Lake Otis, Blueberry Lake," says John. "We'd hitchhike out to Lake Spenard if we had a good, clear freeze with no snow. We set up ski jumps. There was basketball in the community building. Every Christmas, the Elks put on a big party for all the kids in town. We'd all get a stocking with an orange and an apple in it and a bunch of hard candy and they'd treat us to a movie. That was a big thing."

For spending money in winter, John and a friend "struck up a pretty good deal with the girls along the line. We'd go out and get rabbits and ptarmigan and we'd sell them to the girls, 75 cents for ptarmigan, rabbits for 50 cents."

In 1935, John's father built a new, two-story house for the family. Marie tended flowers and potted seedlings shipped from Seattle on the large porch. She joined a florists' telegraph-delivery group, FTD, so she could deliver flowers to or from customers nationwide. She did business under the name Flowers By Bagoy.

In March 1940, shortly before his youngest son graduated from high school, the elder Bagoy collapsed in his greenhouse. He died of a heart attack and was buried in the town cemetery. He was 70. During the two decades Bagoy had been in Anchorage, the town had grown but slowly. At the time of his death, change was on the horizon.

In the early 1940s, the military moved into Alaska in force. About the same time, Northwest Orient started airline flights into Anchorage. When Marie Bagoy had begun her business, perishable products including flowers were unavailable in winter. With regular air connections to Seattle, fresh flowers and produce could be had year-round. The Bagoys gave up on vegetables and concentrated on flowers. And with the military influx, there was a big demand for flowers for corsages.

After high school and a stint on the railroad, John got a job surveying for the construction of Elmendorf Field. The military airfield on the edge of town, he says, "that was what really made Anchorage grow." John joined the military in 1942 and fought in the South Pacific. "When I got back in '49, you couldn't find a house or an apartment or any-place to live." Anchorage's civilian population had nearly tripled between 1940 and 1950 and was approaching 12,000. Thereafter, "it was always boom or bust," Bagoy says. There were more military projects, oil strikes on the Kenai Peninsula, in Cook Inlet, on the North Slope.

Marie ran Flowers By Bagoy until 1952, when she turned operations over to her daughter Mary and her husband. Mary's husband died in 1970. A year earlier, the family had sold the business, although the new owners retain the Bagoy name. In 1982, Marie died in Seattle. She was nearly 96.

Peter, the oldest son, built roads for the State of Alaska for 45 years. "Pete helped build all those homestead roads" in Anchorage, John proudly proclaims, "O'Malley, Huffman, DeArmoun. He was in McKinley Park at Wonder Lake. And he built the Denali Highway. He was a general foreman or superinten-dent on most of those projects."

Doris, the oldest daughter, married a boat captain from Norway. Mary, the next oldest, trained as a nurse at Providence Hospital in Seattle before she took over the flower shop from Marie. Eileen, who graduated from high school in 1933, reigned as Miss Anchorage during the Fur Rendezvous of 1937. She worked for the Alaska Railroad and later married an Air Force sergeant. Gabrielle, the youngest daughter, married a bush pilot who later flew for Pan American Airways. John, the youngest, married a Seward girl after the war and ran an electrical wholesale business until he retired. John's interest in family history helped prompt him to spearhead an effort to compile histories for all of Anchorage's pioneer families. He assembled an exhibit now on display in the Anchorage Museum of History and Art.

"They knew hard work," John says of his parents and their generation. "Dad had a job at the railroad and later worked for the city, and still did all that work in the greenhouse. My mother talked broken English but she had a head for business and handled all her own books. And she was a midwife, she delivered I don't know how many kids. They were just plain, old, hard-working people."

The Bagoys of Anchorage: Some of the plain, old, hard-working people who built Alaska.

In the late 1920s, the Bagoy property on Fourth Avenue looked like this. Marie's flower garden in the foreground faced A Street. Fourth Avenue is to the left. The family bought the pair of houses when they arrived in Anchorage in 1921. (Courtesy of the Bagoy family)

Unveiling the History of the Arctic Basin

By Kathy Berry,
Geophysical Institute

Editor's note: *Kathy Berry is the science writer for the Geophysical Institute at the University of Alaska Fairbanks. This article originally appeared in the Geophysical Institute* Quarterly, *Summer 1993.*

An investigation to find out how islands, mountains and rocks formed in a remote part of Russia has uncovered information that may reveal, for the first time, a complete picture of the geologic history of the Arctic Basin.

For three years, scientists at the Geophysical Institute have worked with Russians to ferret out information about how different masses of land ended up in the polar north. Most of the research has been funded by the National Science Foundation and the Russian Academy of Sciences, but some funding has come from oil companies that hope the clearer picture will reveal more potential oil and mineral reservoirs.

The results of the study should contribute to what is known about continental drift, or the theory of plate tectonics, which assumes the earth's surface is composed of large, semirigid plates that shift position by floating across weaker rocks in the mantle. Heat from the earth's interior drives the movement, which prompts earthquakes and volcanic eruptions in active zones around the globe.

As recently as 10 years ago, scientists began to think that much smaller parts of the earth's surface, called terranes, also move relative to each other. Terranes are typically identified as packages of rocks that are fault bounded and seem to have quite different geologic histories than their neighbors.

Terranes were first identified in Alaska but since have been recognized in many other parts of the world including Yakutia, a region in northeastern Russia about the size of India.

Geophysical Institute research in Yakutia is an extension of work that has been done in Alaska for two decades. Before free access into Russia was permitted, studies of terranes and other geologic features had to be cut off at the Bering Sea. "Going to Russia was the logical next step," said Professor of Geophysics David Stone, the principal investigator involved in the international research. Stone and Research Professor Kazuya Fujita, co-principal investigator, started the collaboration with Russian scientists at the Yakut Science Center in 1990.

What's in a Rock?

After several field seasons of work, hundreds of rocks have been brought back from Yakutia to Geophysical Institute labs for analysis. To a geologist, rocks can reveal more information about past changes in the earth's surface than can a history book.

In addition to containing minerals and fossils of ancient plants and animals, rocks often contain a record of the ancient magnetic field. Analysis of this record is one of the main tools used to investigate terranes.

When rocks form, they often are magnetized in the direction of the earth's magnetic field. By examining the preserved magnetic field within a rock, scientists can tell where it formed in relation to the ancient magnetic poles. Stone uses a superconducting magnetometer at the Geophysical Institute to test the stability of the magnetic field within rocks collected from Yakutia. The sample is considered stable if the magnetic field within it remains unchanged after being heated in steps to 500 degrees Celsius, (932 degrees Fahrenheit) or more.

In another lab, Assistant Professor of Geophysics Paul Layer determines the age of the rock samples. Layer dates rocks using a derivative of the potassium-argon method, which assigns years to the measured radioactive decay of potassium in a rock. Scientists have dated volcanic rocks as young as 50,000 years and metamorphic rocks as old as 1.8 billion years.

A New Plate and a Pivot Point

By figuring out the age of rocks and their position relative to others in a given area, the investigators have pieced together theories that explain how terranes ended up in Yakutia.

Research reveals that the oldest rocks in Russia lie in its interior and that these rocks move together as a unit known as the Eurasian plate. The Pacific edges of the Eurasian plate are composed of terranes that appear to have traveled much greater distances and to have arrived at their current locales more recently than their interior cousins. Rock samples indicate that terranes in the southernmost part of northeastern Russia arrived at their current positions by rafting across the Pacific Ocean; some appear to have come from as far away as equatorial latitudes.

Theories that explain the arrival of the northernmost terranes in Yakutia are less definitive. However, many scientists think that at one time they rotated away from islands in Canada's high Arctic by pivoting around a point in the Mackenzie River delta near the Yukon and Northwest Territories border. Scientists theorize that this movement formed the Arctic Ocean basin sometime between 100 million and 200 million years ago.

Based on this theory, it seems possible that some of Yakutia's northernmost terranes could be closely related to terranes in arctic Alaska. Studies also have revealed that a huge continental shelf lies under the Eastern Siberian Sea, north of Yakutia. Oil has been discovered on a similar, but smaller shelf, existing off the north coast of Alaska.

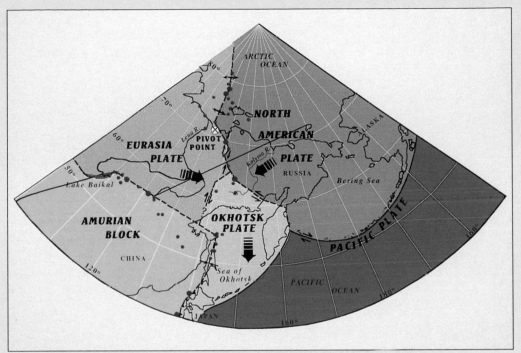

This diagram of the movement of tectonic plates shows selected earthquakes with magnitudes greater than 5 on the Richter scale as recorded between 1960 and 1988, and tectonic plate boundaries as proposed by University of Alaska Fairbanks Geophysical Institute Professor Kazuya Fujita and others. Research indicates the Sea of Okhotsk is being squeezed out into the Pacific Ocean because it lies behind the pivot point of the North American and Eurasian plates. On the opposite side of the pivot point, the two plates are moving apart and enlarging the Arctic Ocean. (Adapted from Fujita et al, 1993, by Deborah Coccia, Geophysical Institute)

However, oil exploration in Yakutia so far has been limited.

Research into the ancient travels of terranes naturally led to studies of present-day plate boundaries. "What is going on today is an indicator of what may have happened in the past," Stone said.

After analyzing Russian records on past earthquakes and setting up seismic stations to assess present-day activity, Fujita, his students and his Russian colleagues made some interesting discoveries. Most important, their research helped draw boundaries around a new plate and it helped pin down the pivot point between the Eurasian and North American plates.

The earth's plates connect through a series of active fault zones in which land masses are pushed apart or pulled together. Fujita set out to find the fault zone that connects the mid-Atlantic ridge to areas of plate convergence on the opposite side of the globe. An extension of the mid-Atlantic ridge, the opening spreading center that pushes apart the North American and Eurasian plates, appears to cross the Arctic Ocean and then to come on shore in northern Yakutia. What was not clear is how the ridge connects to the well-defined plate boundaries of the North Pacific.

Fujita discovered two connections: a curved fault zone that connects the mid-Atlantic ridge in northern Yakutia to Russia's Kamchatka Peninsula, and another relatively straight fault zone that runs from northern Yakutia south to Japan.

These two boundaries define a new plate underlying the Sea of Okhotsk, which appears to be getting squeezed out toward the Pacific Ocean. The compression indicates that the sea lies directly behind the pivot point of the North American and Eurasian plates.

Taku Glacier Thicker Than Reported

Taku Glacier near Juneau is almost a mile thick, not 1,500 feet as was reported in previous studies done in 1949. This new information from a team of Alaska scientists is important for understanding whether Taku Glacier will advance, retreat or remain stationary. These findings also mean that Taku Glacier has the thickest ice as yet reported for any non-polar glacier and is half as thick as the Greenland ice cap. Taku Glacier as advanced four and one-half miles miles since 1890, and its terminus at the end of 1993 lay within one mile of damming the Taku River.

Scientists use seismic sounding techniques to measure glacier thickness, i.e. acoustic signals generated by explosive charges travel through the ice and are reflected from the glacier's bottom. Seismometers detect returning signals, providing a picture of the ice-bedrock channel. Taku's bed lies surprisingly below sea level for much of its length and is 2,000 feet below sea level at its deepest part. Should Taku's ice ever melt, the resulting fiord would rival those found in Glacier Bay and Tracy Arm, both in Southeast.

Dr. Roman Motyka of the Alaska Division of Geological & Geophysical Surveys headed the team of scientists that included Professor Keith Echelmeyer, graduate student Matt Nolan and research assistant Chris Larson, all from the University of Alaska Fairbanks' Geophysical Institute.

The new thickness data helped resolve long standing questions regarding the glacier's mass balance and its flow of ice. The balance is the difference between snow accumulation at higher elevations and ice lost to melting at lower elevations. Ice flowing from higher elevations replenishes ice lost at lower elevations. The ice flowing through a section of channel, calculated using the 1949 ice-thickness measurements, proved to be much too small to account for the glacier's advance. In contrast, the new thickness measurements coincide with what the scientists know about the glacier's mass balance and how the glacier has been growing.

Taku Glacier blocked the Taku River as recently as about 250 years ago. Concern that continued advance of the glacier could block the river again had prompted the current study. The Taku River, a major drainage that flows from British Columbia into Taku Inlet, 20 miles northeast of Juneau, is being considered for an international transportation corridor. The river also hosts commercially important runs of all salmon species.

The advance of Taku Glacier has long puzzled scientists because all neighboring glaciers have been retreating. Motyka and U.S. Geological Survey scientists Austin Post and Dennis Trabant recognized that Taku Glacier was a tidewater-type glacier and attribute its advance to what has been called the "tidewater glacier cycle." Such glaciers undergo periodic rapid retreat followed by gradual readvance. The advance is relatively independent of climate and is a natural part of the cycle that this type of glacier undergoes. Examples of other such glaciers that are advancing are Hubbard Glacier near Yakutat and John Hopkins Glacier in Glacier Bay National Park.

—Alaska Department of Natural Resources, Division of Geological & Geophysical Surveys

Editor's note: *For more information on Alaska's glaciers, see ALASKA GEOGRAPHIC® Vol. 9, No. 1, Alaska's Glaciers, by Dr. Bruce Molnia; for more information on Austin Post and his work with glaciers, see "Ice Maven," by Richard P. Emanuel in the newsletter section of Vol. 19, No. 4, Alaska's Railroads.*

John Muir, Letters from Alaska, edited by Robert Engberg and Bruce Merrell, The University of Wisconsin Press, Madison, 115 pages, 15 black and white illustrations, 3 maps, introduction, chronology, notes on sources, index; hardcover (library binding, no dustjacket) $30; softcover, $12.95.

In 1879 and 1880, naturalist John Muir made extended trips through Southeast Alaska. He came primarily to see the region's glaciers. He explored the waterways by steamship and canoe, often threading ice-clogged passages in pursuit of yet another calving mother lode.

Along the way, Muir preached his "glacial gospel...philosophic sermons that living in and studying nature would transform people," write the editors.

He spent time with the Indians, traveled with the "divines" as he called the missionaries, encountered gold miners and soldiers, visited white settlements. Most of all, he sought nature, and he rejoiced in Alaska's seaside wilderness with the passion of a saved soul.

"And here, too, one easily learns that the world, though made, is yet being made. That this is still the morning of creation," Muir wrote after a day at Baird Glacier near Wrangell, "(We felt) that in very foundational truth we had been to church and had seen God."

Muir wrote and sketched, and he compiled a series of letters sent back on monthly supply

Letters from Alaska

JOHN MUIR

Edited by Robert Engberg and Bruce Merrell

ships for publication in San Francisco's *Daily Evening Bulletin*.

Letters from Alaska presents 14 of Muir's 18 original *Bulletin* dispatches. This slender volume fills a niche in the extensive Muir library by offering, for the first time, the *Bulletin* letters in a single issue for popular consumption. Bits and pieces of these letters may seem familiar, however. Muir excerpted and reworked these letters as part of his book *Travels in Alaska,* widely available and considered a classic of early Alaska writing.

Editors Robert Engberg and Bruce Merrell annotated this collection. Their introduction sketches Muir's life with a discussion of his closely guarded private life, his public role and his devotion to nature. They

also prefaced each letter with interpretative background and interesting asides.

Engberg, social studies department chairman at Mission Bay High School in San Diego, has edited two other collections of Muir writings. Merrell is Alaska bibliographer for Anchorage Municipal Libraries and a director of the Alaska Historical Society.

In his *Bulletin* letters, Muir played scientist, tourist and reporter. As one of the first travelers to Alaska after its purchase from Russia 12 years earlier, he offered glimpses of this relatively new and much maligned acquisition. *Bulletin* readers were somewhat familiar with Muir, who had filed a similar series of articles during earlier travels in California. These articles, particularly those from Yosemite, had engaged the country's emerging conservation ethic.

Muir's subsequent experiences in Alaska catapulted him into leadership of the conservation movement. He was instrumental in the creation of Yosemite National Park, and he started the Sierra Club.

In his later years, Muir started writing a book about Alaska from his various notebooks and articles. He labored over 36 versions of his Alaska tome, yet he was never satisfied and died in 1914 with an unfinished draft on his bed. Eventually one of these manuscripts was published posthumously as *Travels in Alaska.*

Some of Muir's sharpest

observations show up in letters from Fort Wrangel. He contrasted the settlement — "a moist dragglement of unpretentious wooden huts and houses that go wrangling and angling along the boggy, curving shore...the ground in general is a degraded bog, oozy and slimy, too thin to walk in, too thick to swim in..." — with the setting "tranquil as the lovely bay and the islands out-spread in front of it, or the deep evergreen woods behind it."

He wrote vividly about the Natives — women and children selling baskets of berries along the boardwalks and men out fishing and gathering driftwood. The collection shows his changing opinion of the Indians, from condescension at first to admiration, respect and concern.

Muir often found himself with the Presbyterian missionaries, who were in Southeast to convert the Indians. He became friends with one of them, S. Hall Young, and the two traveled with Indian guides in a canoe through the region. Muir saw Indians struggling to maintain their culture. He thought good missionaries could protect Indians from the "degrading vices of civilization." Yet he found the missionaries suspect, and wrote disgustedly of the divines desecrating a totem at an abandoned Indian village. His frank commentaries about the missionaries that appeared in the *Bulletin* were tempered or edited out in the later *Travels.*

—*L.J. Campbell*

BIBLIOGRAPHY

Alaska Department of Fisheries. *Annual Report for 1950*. Report No. 2. Juneau: Alaska Fisheries Board and Alaska Department of Fisheries, 1950.

Alaska Department of Fisheries. *Annual Report for 1951*. Report No. 3. Juneau: Alaska Fisheries Board and Alaska Department of Fisheries, 1951.

Alaska Geographic Society: *Alaska's Salmon Fisheries*, Vol. 10, No. 3, 1983; *The Silver Years*, Vol. 3, No. 4, 1976; *Bristol Bay Basin*, Vol. 5, No. 3, 1978; Anchorage.

Alaska Peninsula and Aleutian Islands Areas Annual Salmon and Herring Management Report, 1991. Regional Information Report No. 4K92-18. Kodiak: Alaska Department of Fish and Game, April 1992.

Alaska Peninsula/Becharof National Wildlife Refuge Complex, Draft, Public Use Management Plan and Environmental Assessment. King Salmon, Alaska: U.S. Fish and Wildlife Service, March 1993.

Alaska Peninsula National Wildlife Refuge, Environmental Impact Statement. Washington, D.C.: U.S. Fish and Wildlife Service, 1980.

Aniakchak National Monument and Preserve, General Management Plan/Environmental Assessment Land Protection Plan, Draft. Washington D.C.: U.S. Dept. of Interior, National Park Service, March 1985.

Annual Management Report, Bristol Bay Area, 1992. Regional Information Report No. 2A93-32. Juneau: Alaska Department of Fish and Game, July 1993.

Annual Management Report for the Shellfish Fisheries of the Westward Region, 1991. Regional Information Report No. 4K92-9. Kodiak: Alaska Department of Fish and Game, March 1992.

Browning, Robert J. *Fisheries of the North Pacific*. Anchorage: Alaska Northwest Publishing Co., 1980.

Fisheries Management Plan Izembek National Wildlife Refuge. Kenai: U.S. Fish and Wildlife Service, Kenai Fishery Resource Office, June, 1993.

Impact Assessment, Inc. *Community Profiles Developed for the Social Impact Assessment of the Inshore/Offshore Amendment Proposal, Sand Point, Alaska*. Anchorage: North Pacific Fishery Management Council, 1991.

Jones, Dorothy M. *Patterns of Village Growth and Decline in the Aleutians*. Institute of Social, Economic and Government Research, Occasional Papers No. 11. Fairbanks: University of Alaska, 1973.

Kodiak Management Area Annual Finfish Management Report, 1991. Regional Information Report No. 4K92-37. Kodiak: Alaska Department of Fish and Game, October 1992.

Minerals Management Service, Alaska Outer Continental Shelf Office, Technical Reports: No. 67, *North Aleutian Shelf Basin Sociocultural Systems Analysis*. November 1983; No. 75, *North Aleutian Shelf, Non-OCS Forecast Analysis*, August 1982; No. 103, *Sociocultural/Socioeconomic Organization of Bristol Bay: Regional and Subregional Analyses*. August 1984; No. 121, *A Sociocultural Description of Small Communities in the Kodiak-Shumagin Region*, 1986.

The Land...The Sea. Sand Point, Alaska: Sand Point High School, 1982.

Tuten, Merry Allyn. *A Preliminary Study of Subsistence Activities on the Pacific Coast of the Proposed Aniakchak Caldera National Monument*. Fairbanks: University of Alaska, 1977.

INDEX (NL denotes an entry found in the newsletter section)

ALASKA GEOGRAPHIC® Back Issues

The North Slope, Vol. 1, No. 1. Charter issue. Out of print.

One Man's Wilderness, Vol. 1, No. 2. Out of print.

Admiralty...Island in Contention, Vol. 1, No. 3. $7.50.

Fisheries of the North Pacific, Vol. 1, No. 4. Out of print.

Alaska-Yukon Wild Flowers Guide, Vol. 2, No. 1. Out of print.

Richard Harrington's Yukon, Vol. 2, No. 2. Out of print.

Prince William Sound, Vol. 2, No. 3. Out of print.

Yakutat: The Turbulent Crescent, Vol. 2, No. 4. Out of print.

Glacier Bay: Old Ice, New Land, Vol. 3, No. 1. Out of print.

The Land: Eye of the Storm, Vol. 3, No. 2. Out of print.

Richard Harrington's Antarctic, Vol. 3, No. 3. $12.95.

The Silver Years, Vol. 3, No. 4. $17.95.

Alaska's Volcanoes: Northern Link In the Ring of Fire, Vol. 4, No. 1. Out of print.

The Brooks Range, Vol. 4, No. 2. Out of print.

Kodiak: Island of Change, Vol. 4, No. 3. Out of print.

Wilderness Proposals, Vol. 4, No. 4. Out of print.

Cook Inlet Country, Vol. 5, No. 1. Out of print.

Southeast: Alaska's Panhandle, Vol. 5, No. 2. Out of print.

Bristol Bay Basin, Vol. 5, No. 3. Out of print.

Alaska Whales and Whaling, Vol. 5, No. 4. $19.95.

Yukon-Kuskokwim Delta, Vol. 6, No. 1. Out of print.

Aurora Borealis, Vol. 6, No. 2. Out of stock.

Alaska's Native People, Vol. 6, No. 3. $24.95.

The Stikine River, Vol. 6, No. 4. $15.95.

Alaska's Great Interior, Vol. 7, No. 1. $17.95.

Photographic Geography of Alaska, Vol. 7, No. 2. Out of print.

The Aleutians, Vol. 7, No. 3. Out of print.

Klondike Lost, Vol. 7, No. 4. Out of print.

Wrangell-Saint Elias, Vol. 8, No. 1. $19.95.

Alaska Mammals, Vol. 8, No. 2. Out of stock.

The Kotzebue Basin, Vol. 8, No. 3. $15.95.

Alaska National Interest Lands, Vol. 8, No. 4. $17.95.

Alaska's Glaciers, Vol. 9, No. 1. Revised 1993. $19.95.

Sitka and Its Ocean/Island World, Vol. 9, No. 2. Out of stock.

Islands of the Seals: The Pribilofs, Vol. 9, No. 3. $15.95.

Alaska's Oil/Gas & Minerals Industry, Vol. 9, No. 4. $15.95.

Adventure Roads North, Vol. 10, No. 1. $17.95.

Anchorage and the Cook Inlet Basin, Vol. 10, No. 2. $17.95.

Alaska's Salmon Fisheries, Vol. 10, No. 3. $15.95.

Up the Koyukuk, Vol. 10, No. 4. $17.95.

Nome: City of the Golden Beaches, Vol. 11, No. 1. $15.95.

Alaska's Farms and Gardens, Vol. 11, No. 2. $15.95.

Chilkat River Valley, Vol. 11, No. 3. $15.95.

Alaska Steam, Vol. 11, No. 4. $15.95.

Northwest Territories, Vol. 12, No. 1. $17.95.

Alaska's Forest Resources, Vol. 12, No. 2. $16.95.

Alaska Native Arts and Crafts, Vol. 12, No. 3. $19.95.

Our Arctic Year, Vol. 12, No. 4. $15.95.

Where Mountains Meet the Sea: Alaska's Gulf Coast, Vol. 13, No. 1. $17.95.

Backcountry Alaska, Vol. 13, No. 2. $17.95.

British Columbia's Coast, Vol. 13, No. 3. $17.95.

Lake Clark/Lake Iliamna Country, Vol. 13, No. 4. Out of print.

Dogs of the North, Vol. 14, No. 1. $17.95.

South/Southeast Alaska, Vol. 14, No. 2. Out of print.

Alaska's Seward Peninsula, Vol. 14, No. 3. $15.95.

The Upper Yukon Basin, Vol. 14, No. 4. $17.95.

Glacier Bay: Icy Wilderness, Vol. 15, No. 1. Out of print.

Dawson City, Vol. 15, No. 2. $15.95.

Denali, Vol. 15, No. 3. $16.95. Out of stock.

The Kuskokwim River, Vol. 15, No. 4. $17.95.

Katmai Country, Vol. 16, No. 1. $17.95.

North Slope Now, Vol. 16, No. 2. $15.95.

The Tanana Basin, Vol. 16, No. 3. $17.95.

The Copper Trail, Vol. 16, No. 4. $17.95.

The Nushagak Basin, Vol. 17, No. 1. $17.95.

Juneau, Vol. 17, No. 2. Out of stock.

The Middle Yukon River, Vol. 17, No. 3. $17.95.

The Lower Yukon River, Vol. 17, No. 4. $17.95.

Alaska's Weather, Vol. 18, No. 1. $17.95.

Alaska's Volcanoes, Vol. 18, No. 2. $17.95.

Admiralty Island: Fortress of the Bears, Vol. 18, No. 3. $17.95.

Unalaska/Dutch Harbor, Vol. 18, No. 4. $17.95.

Skagway: A Legacy of Gold, Vol. 19, No. 1. $18.95.

ALASKA: The Great Land, Vol. 19, No. 2. $18.95.

Kodiak, Vol. 19, No. 3. $18.95.

Alaska's Railroads, Vol. 19, No. 4. $18.95.

Prince William Sound, Vol. 20, No. 1. $18.95.

Southeast Alaska, Vol. 20, No. 2. $19.95.

Arctic National Wildlife Refuge, Vol. 20, No. 3. $18.95.

Alaska's Bears, Vol. 20, No. 4. $18.95.

ALL PRICES SUBJECT TO CHANGE

Your $39 membership in The Alaska Geographic Society includes four subsequent issues of *ALASKA GEOGRAPHIC*®, the Society's official quarterly. Please add $10 for non-U.S. memberships.

Additional membership information is available on request. Single copies of the *ALASKA GEOGRAPHIC*® back issues are also available. When ordering, please make payments in U.S. funds and add $2.00 postage/handling per copy book rate; $4.00 per copy for Priority Mail. Non-U.S. postage extra. Free catalog available. To order back issues send your check or money order or credit card information (including expiration date and daytime telephone number) and volumes desired to:

The Alaska Geographic Society

**P.O. Box 93370
Anchorage, AK 99509**

NEXT ISSUE: *Kenai Country*, Vol. 21, No. 2. South-central Alaska's Kenai Peninsula embraces the traditional Alaska of homesteaders, hunters and fishermen, as well as the modern Alaska fueled by the industries of oil and gas. This economy swirls around the magnificent scenery and striking wildlife that have made the Kenai famous. This issue will look at the region's resources and lifestyle and how they can thrive in light of a growing population and increasing development. To members, 1994, with index. Price $19.95.